THE CHURCH AND MUSIC

VITAE CHRISTIANAE

ARTIS MUSICAE

PRAECEPTORIBUS

PRIMIS OPTIMIS DILECTISSIMIS

JOHN AND ELEANOR ROUTLEY

By the same author

CREEDS AND CONFESSIONS: the Reformation and its
Modern Ecumenical Implications. 1962

THE CHURCH AND MUSIC

An Enquiry into the History, the Nature, and the Scope of Christian Judgment on Music

By

ERIK ROUTLEY

Formerly Mackennal Lecturer in Ecclesiastical History at Mansfield College, Oxford

SOLE U.S. DISTRIBUTOR
CRESCENDO PUB. CO.
48-50 MELROSE ST.
BOSTON, MASS. 02116

GERALD DUCKWORTH & CO. LTD.
3 HENRIETTA STREET, LONDON, W.C.2

Printed in Great Britain
by Photolithography
Unwin Brothers Limited
Woking and London

PREFATORY NOTE

THE first part of this book is based on a thesis submitted in 1946 for the degree of Bachelor of Divinity in Oxford. I have to record my great gratitude to one of my examiners on that occasion, Dr. Percy Scholes, for much valuable help, although I would not leave him with the responsibility for my infelicities. Similarly, I must thank Dr. Nathaniel Micklem for reading the typescript and delivering me from many excesses.

I must take the responsibility for all the translations except those where acknowledgment is made to another translator.

E. R.

Oxford, 1949.

PREFACE TO REVISED EDITION

IT is now twenty-five years since I began the work which eventually resulted in the publication of the first edition of this book in 1950. After such a lapse of time it is not easy to decide how radical a revision ought to be. Those who have read other books which I have since written on subjects akin to this one will have observed that on certain theological and musical

5

points I now take a different position from that which I took when I was less than half as old as I now am. It would be a pretty serious matter if this were not so.

On consideration, I thought the best thing to do was to leave the book very much as it was. I do not disapprove of most of it. If there are things in it which I would now say differently, I have said them in other places. I have entirely revised the final chapter, by adding several paragraphs before and after what I originally wrote, and substituting these for the single opening and closing paragraphs of the original. I have also included a new hymn tune index which takes note of books now current. One or two mistakes in the earlier part of the book I have now corrected.

I hope that those who have called for a new edition are right in thinking that it is not yet quite valueless.

E. R.

Edinburgh, 1966

CONTENTS

PART I

7

CONTENTS—*continued*

PART II

INTRODUCTION

THE purpose of this book is to tell the story of Christian thought about music. In order to give the story a beginning, a little time will have to be spent on the musical judgment and practice of pre-Christian religion and moralism ; and in order to provide an interim conclusion for a necessarily incomplete story, our last pages will be given to a discussion of the proper grounds of Christian judgment on music as they may be deduced from the story itself which, told historically, forms the body of the book.

This is the first time that an attempt has been made to tell the whole story, although certain important chapters in it have already been written. Of these the most notable are *The Puritans and Music*, by Dr. Percy Scholes,[1] and *A History of Byzantine Music and Hymnody*, by Dr. Egon Wellesz.[2] But the reader should be warned that this is not a text book, either of musical or of ecclesiastical history. In these fields we have nothing to add to the work of the many and excellent historians to whose instruction our purely historical pages are entirely in debt. What we shall be examining is the impact of that " supernatural " history which is church-history on that " natural " history which is the history of music ; we shall be drawing out the implications of the truth that the human race was born singing but was not born Christian.

[1] Oxford University Press, 1936.
[2] O.U.P., 1949.

9

Introduction

One effect of the ambiguous nature of our subject matter on the form of this work will be a notable lack of homogeneity. The reader will probably be disconcerted by an alternation of large-scale generalisation with occasional technical minuteness. For this we apologise now by saying that it has seemed that a readable story will best be achieved if we summarise in as general a way as accuracy permits the work of the musical and ecclesiastical historians on whom we lean so heavily, but devote some time and care to the working of those sections in which we seem to be breaking new ground. What is familiar or readily accessible to the reader we summarise, referring him to the authorities for the details. What is probably unfamiliar we treat in detail. Thus we summarise the musical apprehensions of the Old Testament, but give more extensive quotations from the less-known passages in Plato and Aristotle ; we sketch in lightly the background of church-history up to the Renaissance, but we feel justified in treating Augustine's *De Musica* more technically than any other section of the book. Dr. Scholes, in the work we have mentioned, saves us much labour in the seventeenth century, but we have felt that the nineteenth requires new and careful analysis. Contemporary music and musical criticism are within arm's reach of the reader, but the musical metaphysic of Heinrich Schenker has so strangely small a hearing and such immediate relevance to our subject that, even at so late a stage as our final chapter, we must attend to it with patience.

We shall tell the story with as little technical language as possible, because we hope that it will be attended to by theologians and musicians whose sympathy with each other's subject may extend to good will but falls short of direct knowledge. We write under the conviction that if the purpose of the Origin and Creator of both is to be fulfilled, the relation between music and theology should be one not of suspicion, contempt, or patronage, but of courtesy.

CHAPTER I

THE PRE-CHRISTIAN BACKGROUND OF MUSICAL CRITICISM

Music in primitive communities—Music in the Bible—Theoretic Developments in Greece—Plato, the beginning of criticism—Aristotle, counter-criticism—From Greece to Rome.

(*a*) MUSIC IN PRIMITIVE COMMUNITIES

The following facts are clear about the development of music during the ages preceding the Christian era :

1. It has been an activity *natural* to man from the first.

2. As soon as man was capable of those exalted and even ecstatic modes of life which can be gathered under the term " religious ", music is found to be closely associated with those modes.

3. But in one area of pre-Christian civilisation, namely, Greece, music was observed to be not only associated with ecstasy but also to be (*a*) a branch of metaphysics and (*b*) subject to moral judgment.

The first two of these points scarcely need amplifying. All the evidence gathered by the scholars in anthropology and comparative religion, and by the pioneers on the mission field, shows that music of a primitive but recognisable kind is not only a natural activity of man at all stages of his development, but is peculiarly natural to that region of consciousness which we call religious. Music here means, of course, no more than melody and bass of the most

13

elementary kind. It is well known, for example, that in India music is associated with religious exaltation, and that this music consists of a steady, monotonous pulsation sustained by percussion instruments, and a wayward, ecstatic melody sung or played above it.[1] There is no internal connection between the melody and the pulsation, such as there is in modern music of the West ; the effect indeed is not of melody shaped and disciplined by rhythm, but of a melody (containing its own rhythm) doing furious battle with the pulsations of the drums like a bird dashing itself against a window-pane. Scholars have already pointed out that this tension is symbolic of the tension in oriental religion between the One and the Many, the static and the wayward, the timeless Negative and the temporal vitality. We shall have to refer to this matter again, but we mention it here only to show that in India music and religious ecstasy are complementary. Moreover, and this is most important, music even of this primitive form is already a language without words, a non-verbal vehicle of expression. In the section that follows it will be seen how music becomes a vehicle not only for emotion but also for continuous thought ; not only ecstasy but also *argument*.

(*b*) THE BIBLE

Parallels to this statement about Indian music can be adduced from all over the world ; we may mention in passing the melody-and-drone technique of the bagpipes, where the drone takes the place of

[1] A suggestive application of this truth is to be found in N. Micklem, *Religion* (1948), pp. 47 f.

the regular percussive pulsation, and we must resist the temptation to enlarge on the strange incursion of this same technique into the sophisticated twentieth-century ballroom.[1] If it be conceded that primitive music is natural and proper to ecstatic conditions of mind, whether religious or otherwise, we find that the Old Testament confirms this view. It is, for instance, no far-fetched fancy that causes the author of *Job* to say that at the creation the morning stars " sang " together,[2] and the Psalmist to tell of the hills and valleys "singing ".[3] Music to these ancient poets was of the very fabric of the universe ; it was the expression of joy in living, of gratitude for the Creator's love. Moreover, we find in the most primitive parts of the Old Testament records of prophets and (perhaps especially) prophetesses breaking into song at exalted moments, as did Miriam and Deborah, Hannah and David.[4] Even if this " song " was no more than an exalted and stylised sort of oratory, none the less it is taken for song by those who recorded it, who would otherwise have called it speech ; and even if none of these primitive odes is to be properly ascribed to its reputed author, we must believe that those who so ascribed them did at any rate think that what they call

---

[1] It is a wild misuse of a language to call this " rhythm " because rhythm (ῥυθμός) means a " flow ", while the implication of this regular pulsation is, by origin and use, the static and the immovable, and the effect of this form of music is the primitive tension between the movement of a restless melody and the inexorable stability of the bass. " Rhythm " can, on the other hand, be properly applied to plain song melodies which know nothing of regular pulsations.

[2] Job, xxxviii. 7.

[3] Ps. lxv. 13. Cf. xcviii. 4, xcvi. 11 f., Isa. xlix. 13.

[4] Ex. xv, Jud. v, I Sam. 11, II Sam. i. Cf. the Gospel Canticles, Lk. i. 46, i. 68, ii. 14, ii. 29.

15

" song " was not out of place at such moments, which is all we require at present. And in that strange prophecy which is known to us as *Revelation* it is not the lapse of an otherwise clear-headed and accurate author into woolly melodrama that causes so many references to the music of the heavenly Community ; on the contrary, he seems to have felt very strongly that the inexpressible, which is for ever on the lips of the redeemed, can only be done justice by music. Even the voice of the angel is " like a trumpet ".[1]

Two other aspects of Biblical music must be mentioned, of which the first is the *liturgical*. The Psalter, of course, implies the liturgical music which forms the basis of synagogue-music to this day, and which was the basis of the first Christian church music. Paul's " psalms and hymns and spiritual music "[2] falls into this category ; the " hymn "[5] sung by Jesus and His friends after the Last Supper was part of it ; and those passages in the New Testament[4] which are regarded as fragments of Christian hymns are, if properly so regarded, new words set to the traditional tunes, a Christian adaptation of a Jewish use. This liturgical music was exceedingly primitive in technique, consisting only of a broad unison melody of a few notes, more primitive, less melodic, nearer to speech than the simplest of Christian plainsong. But it may be observed that the drone-bass has disappeared. The celebrated orchestra in Daniel iii. 15 contains nothing

---

[1] Rev. iv. 1. Cf. v. 11-13.

[2] Eph. v. 19 (Knox).

[3] Mk. xiv. 26.

[4] Eph. v. 14, I Tim. iii. 16, I Tim. vi. 15 f, II Tim. ii. 11 ff, Titus iii. 4-7, Phil. ii. 5-11, Rev. xv. 3-4, Rev. xxii. 17.

more percussive than a dulcimer. It is melody that is foremost, and the restraining discipline is now the words to which it is set. Dancing before the Lord gives place to decorous choristry ; the ecstatic tension of the barbarian band is replaced by the severe mono-tone and cadence of Hebrew cantillation.

The other aspect of music which forces itself on our notice from the pages of the Bible is that implied in the story of David's charming away Saul's madness by performing on the harp.[1] Orpheus and Arion in mythology charm nature ; to this day snake-charmers employ the same technique. Here we have deliberate action on the assumption that music has not only power to speak but the transitive power to *act*. The Fathers of the Church and the medieval musicologists returned again and again to this story because of its implications.

In Scripture, then, we see music, if not fully grown, at any rate fully formed *in potentia*. It is, though its possibilities are almost all still latent, nothing less than a form of word or ' logos '—natural to man, expressive of human emotions, potent over human beings, and, as the Greeks showed, a vehicle of Reason.

(c) THEORETIC DEVELOPMENTS IN GREECE.[2]

A more extended treatment of Greek thought on music is justified not only by the relative inaccessi-bility of the sources but also by the vital importance of the thought of the Greeks, especially Plato and Aristotle, to early Christian thought. It was in Greek categories that the public pronunciations of Christian doctrine were eventually cast, and it will

[1] I Sam. xvi. 23 ff.
[2] On this subject see Wellesz, *op. cit.*, Ch. II.

be clear from what we have to say that the Greek metaphysic and science of music as well as Greek criticism lead straight into the early Christian judgments with which our second chapter will be occupied.

Two words we would select from the vocabulary of Greek philosophy as relevant to this study ; they are *theoria* and *harmonia*. To translate them " theory " and "harmony" would leave everything of importance unsaid. We must paraphrase.

Theoria[1] is the activity of contemplating what Aristotle called the " thing in itself ".[2] That is what we might call " objective thinking " or " abstract thinking ". Its exercise requires a severe mental discipline in order that the forces which prejudice, association, emotion, and sloth exert on the mind may be negatived. The word " contemplation " is a satisfactory translation only if the reader does not follow the general disposition of modern Englishmen to regard contemplation as a species of sleep or coma. It was this faculty for seeing what is really there and for dismissing what is irrelevant and distorting to the vision that the Greek philosophers from Pythagoras[3] to Aristotle[4] cultivated, and when they applied it to music they found that music responded readily to reasonable examination and therefore right by concluded that it was itself reasonable by nature.

Harmonia[5] expresses in a word the Greek predisposition of mind which lay behind the activity of

---

[1] θεωρία.
[2] τὸ τί ἦν εἶναι
[3] Fl. B.C. 510.
[4] B.C. 384–322.
[5] ἁρμονία.

theoria and (in spite of all efforts to the contrary) conditions its findings. Its modern philosophical translation is, roughly, " monism ". It is the principle of integration, the outlook which sees Reality as a single whole, in which all contraries are resolved and in which all movement is brought to rest. One of the epithets used for this one and undifferentiated reality by the school of Pythagoras was a newly-coined compound word meaning " male and female ".[1] On this view the phenomenal world was a world in tension of movement and differentiation which was in process of being resolved into the undifferentiated and motionless One. *Harmonia* is the characteristics property of this monistic universe. It is what scientists now call the " principle of economy ", and its literal translation is " the quality of fittingness ". (A moral theory superimposed on this by Christians of the Greek school identified movement and contrariety with the state of sin brought about by the Fall.)

If, then, the activity of *theoria* led the Greek philosophers to cultivate an unparalleled skill in detecting the truth, the presupposition of *harmonia* caused them to seek relations, connections, and parallels between all phenomenal categories. Nothing could be more opportune, then, for this earliest school of Greek philosophy, than the discovery that between music and mathematics there was an inescapable connection. From the discovery[2] that two strings vibrating, the one twice as frequently as the other, produce the plainest concord in music, a scientific

[1] ἀρσενοθῆλυς, (Plutarch, *Moralia II*, 368c).

[2] Nichomachus of Gerasa, in his *Harmonikon Encheiridion*, ascribes this discovery to Pythagoras.

theory was worked out which came to its first full fruit
in the work of Aristoxenus.[1] In the first musical
scientists, then music is not an art but a science ;
it is the vehicle, not of emotion but of reason.

(d) PLATO—THE BEGINNING OF CRITICISM

But much more interesting and controversial is the
relation which Plato held to exist between music and
the moral world. Here we are observing music
once more as the primitives saw it—expressive and
potent. The contemplative Greek mind, at its zenith
in Plato and Aristotle, accepting music's emotional
content and its potency, immediately asks " Expressive of what ? " " Potent over whom and to what
end ? " ; and it finds the answers—" Expressive of
good and evil things ", and " Potent over men for
good or evil ". This answer we must here treat as
settled ; argument about its truth belongs elsewhere.
Its consequences in Plato's political and moral theory
must, however, engage our attention.

A quotation from the *Laches* makes a good starting-
point. It is not a piece of musical criticism, but it
will serve as a reminder of Plato's approach to the
subject.

" When I hear a man discussing virtue, or any
kind of wisdom, one who is truly a man and worthy
of his argument, I am highly delighted. I take
the speaker and his speech together, and observe
how they consort and harmonise together. Such
a man is exactly what I understand by " musical "
—he has tuned himself with the finest harmonies,

[1] fl. 318 B.C.

not that of a lyre or other instrument of amusement, but has made a true concord of his own life
between his words and his deeds, not in the Ionian
nor in the Phrygian, nor in the Lydian, but simply
in the Dorian mode, which is the one and only
Hellenic harmony."[1]

Observe from these words first Plato's acceptance of
the fundamental presupposition of *harmonia*. Musical
harmonia and personal integrity are collateral species
of the architectonic *harmonia* of reality. This is the
" scientific " aspect of music still. But when Plato
in his last sentence says that the Dorian mode is the
one and only Hellenic harmony, he means, as we shall
see, more than that it is the only mode which takes
its name from a state in the Balkan Peninsula.

When we turn to the *Republic* and the *Laws* we
find criticism, not to say censorship. The central
theme of the *Republic* is not, of course, politics, but the
supreme good of man. This Plato believes to be
achieved by what he calls the " harmony of the soul "
(of which the foregoing quotation gives a hint). In
order to show what this means, Socrates, the chief
spokesman of the *Republic*, postulates a " model city "
which in its diversity of citizens he uses as an allegory
of the human personality with its diversity of passions
and impulses. Whether or not Plato (or Socrates)
becomes so interested in this model community that
its component citizens come embarrassingly to life
and thus create a fresh order of problems to obscure
the final purpose of the whole picture remains a
matter for philosophical debate ; on the result of that

[1] Laches, 188 c-d.

debate, which we will not conduct here, it depends how seriously we take the politics, as distinct from the psychology, of the *Republic*.   But it is in the course of his study of the discipline of the community that Plato makes the first of his striking comments on music.

The argument[1] may be summarised thus.   " We may accept the fact that some kinds of literature are liable to conduce to good morals and others to bad morals ; if some of even our most treasured classics fall into the latter category, they must go. Very well.   The same must apply to music. Some modes of music conduce to the martial virtues, and some to the contemplative virtues ; others are depressing and enervating. We find, indeed, that only one mode is of value for the martial virtues and one for the contemplative. Then the rest must go. And we must keep a strict watch to ensure that the prohibited modes do not find their way in." Thus the principle of censorship is established, and the operative factor is the " mode " of the music. The approved modes are, in fact, the Dorian for the martial temper and the Phrygian for the contemplative. (In the Gregorian system with which we are familiar, these are respectively the " authentic " forms of the Phrygian and Dorian modes, E-E and D-D). The importance of this argument is obviously not in its method of criticism. It is not, of course, so bad as saying that only the keys of D minor and E minor are suitable for the use of composers ; that would be a different kind of assertion, since the technical device of transposition, or the repetition of a given mode from different keynotes, has no place in the ancient musical

[1] *Republic* III. 10 (398 c–399 c) and IV. 3 (424 b-c).

scheme. It is, however, much more like saying that all music written in minor keys is pernicious (or like the more familiar fiction that all minor keys are mournful), and it errs in basing its criticism on a property of the music which belongs not to the moral sphere at all but to the scientific. None the less, in as much as it assumes the expressiveness and potency of music, and also its status as a force to be considered seriously, this argument is not without foundation.

But it is in the *Laws*, an avowedly political treatise which dispenses with the humanising influence of Socrates, that Plato is heard at his most ruthless. Still arguing from the same premises, he goes into the matter of state control and censorship of music in some detail. Speaking here of music in the widest sense, that is, anything which comes under the purview of the Muses (what we generically call " art "), Plato says[1] that the judge of music should have regard to three categories—(*a*) utility, or moral effect, (*b*) correctness, or technical quality, and (*c*) " charm " or pleasure-content. Pleasure, he adds, is a natural concomitant of correctness and utility, but of itself no criterion. Then he continues,[2] in respect of music in the narrower sense, by indicating the sources of badness[3] in music. He mentions, first, incongruity between music and words, second, improper and undisciplined complexity and flamboyance, and third, anything that is what he calls " clownish ", and exhibits a " craving for speed, mechanical dexterity, and the imitation of the sounds of animals ".

[1] Laws 667 b–669 b.
[2] Ib. 669 b-e.
[3] τὸ χαλεπόν.

In another place[1] he expresses his impatience with the
fastidious distinctions which musicians are apt to pre-
suppose in referring to a piece of music as " well-
coloured "[2] insisting that those tunes[3] which refer to
goodness of soul or body are universally good,
while those which refer to evil are just bad in a way
that needs no qualification.

Since these are his views, Plato does not hesitate to
advise censorship and state-control. Three passages
now to be quoted will sufficiently expound this view.

" In the matter of music the people used to submit willingly to orderly control, and abstained from
the impudent practice of judging by clamour ; but
later on, with the progress of time, there arose certain
poets who though not without poetry in their
natures were ignorant of what was right and lawful
in music ; the result was the abandonment of
discipline and the destruction of musical taste. Inspired to the point of frenzy and unduly possessed
by a spirit of pleasure seeking, they confused dirges
and praise, paens and dithyrambs, gave to the
harp music appropriate to the flute, and in general
confused all proper distinctions and definitions in
music ; by such behaviour, the product of folly
rather than malice, they falsely represented music
as an art with no standard of correctness, of which
the best criterion is the pleasure of the auditor,
whether he be a man of good or bad judgment.
By compositions of this kind, set to similar words,
they encouraged in the people an attitude of lawless-
ness towards music, and the impudent notion that

[1] Ib. 654 e–657 c.
[2] εὔχρων. [3] σχήματα

they were themselves competent to pass judgments on it. And so the theatre-goers, once decorously silent, now clamorously asserted their right to judge between good and bad music ; in place of an aristocracy in music there arose a ' theatocracy '. Now if in music alone there had arisen this democracy[1] of free men, we should have little cause for alarm ; but the fact is that the universal conceit of universal wisdom and the contempt for authority with which we are familiar has its origin in the realm of music, and it has been followed by licence anarchy. For these people, thinking themselves good judges, abandoned discipline and proceeded from audacity to effrontery ; for to be fearless of the opinion of a better man through self-conceit is nothing less than effrontery[2] of the basest kind. This is what comes of such shameless licence."[3]

Plato here shows the philosopher's lordly contempt for popular judgments. The remedy which he proposed for this serious situation is described in the following passage.

" Our contention is, then, that every means must be employed not only to prevent our children from desiring to copy alien models in dancing or singing, but further to prevent anyone from tempting them to do so by any kind of pleasurable inducement. . . . To attain this end, no better device is likely to come to hand than that of the Egyptians ; I

---

[1] The reader is reminded that in Plato " democracy " is a word of ontempt.

[2] θράσος

[3] *Laws* 700 d.

refer to the practice of consecrating[1] all music and
dancing. Our statesmen should begin by drawing
up an annual list of the feasts to be held, with their
dates and their appropriate deities. . . . Next
they must ordain which hymn is to be sung at each
of the religious sacrifices, and with which dances
each occasion is to be adorned. . . . Then, if
any man propose other hymns or dances for any
celebration, the priests and priestesses will be acting
in accordance with both religion and law if, with the
help of the police, they expel him from the festival ;
any man who resists expulsion should be liable for
the rest of his life to public prosecution for
sacrilege."[2]

This passage is closely followed by an utterance
which is not without prophetic content :

" As for the songs and dances, this is the way in
which they should be arranged. Among the compositions of the ancients there exist many fine old
pieces of music, and dances likewise, from which
we may select without scruple for the constitution
we are founding such as are fitting and proper.
To examine these and make the selection, we shall
select men not under fifty years of age, and whichever of the ancient songs they approve we shall
adopt, but whichever fail to reach our standard,
or are altogether unsuitable, we shall either reject
entirely, or revise and remodel. For this purpose
we shall call in the advice of poets and musicians,
and make use of their poetical ability, without,
however, trusting to their tastes or their wishes,

[1] καθιέρωσαι.
[2] *Laws* 798 f.

except in rare instances ; and by thus expounding the intentions of the lawgiver, we shall organise to his satisfaction dancing, singing, and the whole of choristry. In truth every· unregulated musical pursuit becomes, when brought under regulation, a thousand times better, even when no honeyed strains are served up ;[1] all alike provide pleasure. For if a man has been reared from childhood up to the age of steadiness and sense in the use of music that is sober and regulated, then he detests the opposite kind whenever he hears it, and calls it "vulgar "[2] : whereas, if he has been reared up in tbe common hackneyed type of music, he declares the opposite of this to be cold and unpleasing."[3]

And failure in the recommended vigilance produces this :

" In our part of the world this is what happens, one may say, in almost every one of the states· Whenever a magistrate holds a public sacrifice, the next thing is for a crowd of choirs—not merely one —to advance and take their stand, not at a decent distance from the altars, but often quite close to them : and then they let out a flood of blasphemy over the sacred offerings, exciting the souls of the audience with words, rhythms, and tunes most bewitching, and the man that succeeds at once in drawing most tears from the sacrificing city carries off the palm of victory. Must we not reject such a custom as this ? "[4]

[1] παρατιθεμένης·
[2] ἀνελευθέρον: " unworthy of a free man."
[3] *Laws* 802 a-d.
[4] *Laws* 800 c-d.

From all this Plato feels entitled to conclude that

"The poet shall compose nothing which goes beyond the limits of what the state holds to be fair, legal, right, and good."[1]

In estimating the value of this uncompromising contribution to the history of musical criticism two things must be borne in mind. The first is that Plato regards music and all art as situated on the lowest epistemological plane. Dividing the epistemological universe into two halves, between which the relation is as of shadow to substance or reflection to reality, he subdivides each half under the same relation ; so that in the lower half we have the phenomenal world in the prior position and the aesthetic world (which he sometimes calls " mimetic " or " imitative ") in the lower. Art, therefore, is to him a reflection of a reflection, and as such is, from the philosopher's point of view, the least reliable of all vehicles of truth. The philosopher in Plato, therefore, deals with art with a high hand, and the politician or " lawgiver ", the real " hero " of the *Laws*, carries out his instructions.

Secondly, whenever Plato has music in mind in a civic context, he is thinking of it as it was used on religious occasions, and especially in that religious occasion which was celebrated with drama. Hence his remarks about congruity between words and music, and his invective against extravagance in public performances. We must therefore distinguish between the more theoretical argument in the *Republic*, where the modes are linked up with moral categories, and the more practical argument here, where he is concerned

[1] Ib. 801 c.

with musical abuses of a specific kind. This distinction will be met with again in the course of this study and reflected in the two forms of criticism which we shall encounter—that which deals with music as an object of enquiry in its own right, and that which deals with the practical use of music in church. It is clear, of course, that Plato is on shaky ground when he is discussing music abstractly, and it is possible to say that in the *Laws* his impatience with the judgments not only of the " people " but also of the musicians themselves weakens his case. But, of course, given his standards of criticism, he is entitled to lay down such principles for the use of music on public occasions as may follow from them.

But this cavalier treatment of music and musicians reflects the high respect which Plato had for the potency of music. He was always aware that the appeal of music was universal, and that its capacity if not to declare at any rate to reflect ultimate realities, good or evil, was a force to be reckoned with. " Education in music ", he says in the *Republic*,[1] " is the most sovereign because more than anything else rhythm and harmony find their way to the inmost soul, and take the strongest hold upon it, bringing with them and imparting a right mind[2] if one is rightly trained, and otherwise the contrary." And again, near the end of the *Laws*, he has this :

" [The god-fearing man must grasp] that reason which, as we have often affirmed, controls the heavenly order, together with the necessary preliminary sciences : and he must observe also the

[1] *Republic* III 410 d.
[2] εὐσχημοσύνη.

connexion therewith of musical theory, and apply it harmoniously to the institutions and rules of ethics."[1]

It is on this foundation, as we shall see, that Augustine built the remarkable edifice of his *De Musica*.

(e) ARISTOTLE—COUNTER-CRITICISM

Aristotle's criticism of the views expressed by Plato raises another issue which will recur in succeeding chapters. Where Plato is authoritarian, Aristotle is liberal in his politics, and up to a point the same distinction may be seen in their philosophies. Aristotle carried on the philosophical activity of *theoria* from Plato,[2] and the results of his searches, as they are preserved to us in his lecture-notes, are remarkable. That central attention which Plato give to the timeless " universal ", Aristotle directs upon the " thing in itself "—not by any means giving priority to the phenomenal world, but directing his enquiry rather to the particular and practical than to the universal.[3] Aristotle prefers, for example in the *Nicomachean Ethics*, to examine accepted standards of conduct and see how they are related to the universal Goodness. His celebrated doctrine of the " mean " is not a doctrine of compromise but one of practical *harmonia*. Speaking of courage, for example, he has two things to say—first that courage in general

[1] *Laws* 967 d-e.

[2] Plato's dates are 429–347, Aristotle's, 384–322.

[3] This statement would have to be modified if (*a*) this were a textbook on philosophy, and (*b*) as much of Aristotle as of Plato were preserved to posterity. But if we had considered it misleading we should not have made it.

is the resultant of two forces, discretion and boldness, whose excess leads to pusillanimity and bravado respectively ; and second, that courage on a particular occasion is the right admixture of these elements with reference to that occasion. Right conduct, therefore, has to be considered not abstractly but always in a particular context.[1] A right act is the proper balance, or harmony, between two forces which work from opposite directions. The importance of this outlook for musical criticism will be immediately clear.

But his criticism of Plato is not founded only upon this, nor is it merely destructive, for Aristotle contributes to the discussion a revolutionary theory of aesthetics. So much of his *Poetics* is lost that it is unwise to attribute an aesthetic system to him in too much detail. But enough of it remains to leave us with a clear impression of his doctrine of *catharsis*, or " purgation ". The conclusion of his ethical argument, that the good life is a matter of right proportion, the resultant of well-balanced forces, becomes the major premise of a new argument whose conclusion is that it is the business of all art to restore this " balance " in man's distorted personality. The process of elimating excess in one or other component force he calls *catharsis*. He holds, further,[2] that in achieving this end art must amuse,[3] must command intellectual attention,[4] and must tend towards virtue.[5] He is well aware that the chief danger is that the

---

[1] The distinction is expressed in the *Nicomachean Ethics* as between μέσον τοῦ πράγματος and μέσον πρὸς ἡμᾶς.

[2] *Politics* VIII, iv. 1 (1339 a).

[3] παίδια.

[4] διαγώγη καὶ φρόνησις.   [5] παιδεία.

pleasure-content of art may become an end in itself, but his comment in the *Nicomachean Ethics* upon pleasure says the last word on this matter.

> " Pleasure perfects the activity, not as the fixed disposition does by being already present in the agent, but as a supervening perfection, like the bloom of health on the young and vigorous."[1]

He further acutely observes that men are the more ready to pursue this pleasure-content because the educative function of art, the third of the duties mentioned above, is a " painful " process.[2]

He agrees wholly with Plato that music has great power, and that it has vital connections with morality. He is, indeed, happy to accept the connections already established between certain modes and certain moral and emotional conditions, but the conclusion he draws would have surprised Plato.

> " Since we accept the classification of melodies made by our philosophers . . . distributing the various harmonies[3] among these classes as being in nature akin to one or the other, and as we say that the use of music may be justified by reference not to a single possible benefit but to several (for it serves the purposes of education, purgation, and amusement . . .), it is clear that we are entitled to make use of all the modes, but not all in the same way ; that is we should use the more ethical ones for education, and the active and ecstatic ones for listening when others are performing (for any

[1] *N.E.* X, iv. 8 (1174 *ad fin.*).
[2] *Politics* VIII, iv. (1339 a 29).
[3] I.e. *modes.*

experience which occurs violently in some souls is to be found, though with differing degrees of intensity, in all.)"[1]

From this Aristotle passes to direct criticism of Plato :

" Socrates in the *Republic*[2] is wrong to allow only the Phrygian and Dorian modes, especially when he has disqualified the flute among instruments ; for the Phrygian among the modes and the flute among the instruments have an identical moral force, being violently exciting and emotive. . . . There are, in fact, two objects to which we must constantly attend—the possible and the suitable. We must give preference to the things that are possible, and to those of the possible things that are suitable for the particular class of people with whom we are concerned.[3] We shall find that in these decisions we have to reckon with the dividing lines drawn by age ; people for example, whose powers have faded through the passing of time cannot easily sing the highly-strung harmonies, and for them nature suggests the " relaxed "[4] harmonies. . . . And so some musical experts rightly criticise Socrates because, attributing to the relaxed modes the quality of intoxication (by which he intended not exaltation but exhaustion), he disqualified them for the purposes of education. These modes are, however, appropriate to the older generation, and can

[1] *Politics* VIII, vii. 4-5 (1341 b).

[2] 399 a (see page 21f).

[3] This is an application of the doctrine of the Mean referred to on page 30f.

[4] ἀνειμένας.

C

be used by the elderly without the least discredit. . . . We should lay down these three canons to guide our education—the moderate, the possible, and the fitting."[1] [2]

Aristotle wants right music as much as Plato, but will not admit Plato's wholesale rejection of certain modes or certain instruments, although he is prepared to admit that the flute is singularly liable to abuse. Despite his liberality, however, Aristotle wishes to see laws framed to discourage the bad and cultivate the good.[3] All musical criticism must be conducted according to his two canons—the theoretic and the practical mean. All categories of art can be good, all bad ; everything depends on how they are composed and how used.[4]

(f) FROM GREECE TO ROME, 323 B.C. TO A.D. 30

Three and a half centuries separate the death of Aristotle from Pentecost, and the most obvious development during this period is the shift of the centre of political gravity from Greece to Rome. While Aristotle was delivering some of his later lectures at Athens, a brilliant young pupil of his named Alexander was converting Greece almost overnight from an aggregation of autonomous and mutually belligerent

---

[1] τὸ μέσον, τὸ δυνάτον, τὸ πρέπον.

[2] *Politics* VIII, vii. 9, 12 ff. (1342 a-b).

[3] Ib. 1341 a ad fin.

[4] Both Platonic and Aristotelian influences can be seen in the work of the second-century theorist, Cleonides, who distinguishes three " echoi " in music—stimulating, depressing, and soothing, which he says are respectively proper to Tragedy, Lamentation, and Religious music. (Wellesz, op. cit., p. 44.)

city-states into something like a Great Power. During his brief reign of thirteen years[1] Alexander of Macedon stretched the boundaries of a new empire from southern Italy to India. His preceptor outlived him by a year, but no hint of power-politics ever found its way into Aristotle's teaching. To the end he lectured from the basis of the ancient city-state, and Alexander's politics remained a foreign language to him and to the Greek genius in general. For Alexander was founding not the Greek empire but the Roman empire.

When Perseus, king of Macedon, was defeated by L. Aemilius Paulus at Pydna in 168 B.C., the territory of Alexander's conquests became formally Roman territory. It was then clear that Alexander had ploughed up the ground in which Greek culture could be sown, and around which the organising genius of Rome could with little difficulty erect a fence. The Roman genius working on a world made smaller and more manageable by improved communications, both commercial and intellectual, soon made of this widespread area a very solid empire. It is not unimportant to observe this difference between the Roman and the Greek character ; it can be seen clearly in the earlier history of both communities. While the Greeks were at the height of a civilisation based on maritime trade and academic enquiry (that is, in the sixth and fifth centuries), Rome was a comparatively obscure community of landowners and peasants whose instincts were all towards the land and the spirits of their forefathers. It is not insignificant, indeed, that the one civilisation bears the name of a whole country, while the other, less imaginative, more

[1] 336–323 B.C.

disciplined and authoritarian, is always associated with a single city.

It was the Punic Wars[1] which caused Rome to "find itself" as a military power, and left the legions with a strip of conquered territory in North Africa and the confidence to face the Macedonian might. Therefore, what became just before the opening of the Christian era the Roman *imperium*[2] was the result of a strange and mighty conpromise between the cast-iron immobility of Roman grandeur and the leaping, "contemplative" resources of Greece. Rome had taken over the Olympian hierarchy of Greek public religion and now found in it a serviceable vehicle for demonstrations of totalitarian high-mindedness ; Athens became the university of the Roman world, and the Roman of patrician rank was glad to add a little philosophy to his accomplishments. The literary minds of Rome adopted Greek poetic forms—the epic, the comedy, the epigram, the ode, and the bucolic. In the partnership Greece remained the inventor, Rome the disposer.

But inevitably there remained elements in both parties which were not soluble in this compromise. Although Greece and Rome shared their public religion, the Roman never abandoned the worship of his *lares and penates*, the "household gods", nor dishonoured the sanctity of the *focus*, the hearth. No less tenaciously did the Greeks abide by their "mysteries", those exuberant fantasies which were the real core of the Greek's personal religion. What Rome added in literature was the satire of Juvenal ;

[1] 264–241 and 218–201 B.C.

[2] This is to date the *imperium* from the Augustan settlement, 27 B.C.

what she added in religion was the sanctification of the *Salus populi Romani*, and the farce of emperor-worship which gave Vespasian the occasion for a death-bed joke and Domitian the occasion for much sadistic indulgence. Even if Virgil may stand beside Homer, Cicero beside Demosthenes, and Martial beside the Greek Anthology, there is only one answer to a comparison between the laborious bawdry of Plautus and the sparkling grace (in its place no less bawdy) of Aristophanes. And here, perhaps, is the whole secret of the difference between the new Power and the old. Greece had not only wisdom but also humour. Rome could rise to nothing beyond academic wit. Who can imagine Cato behaving under sentence of death as Socrates is reported in the *Phaedo* to have borne himself? The Greeks never lost their faculty for " self-emptying " humour. The Roman key-word was *gravitas*.

This brings us to the second strand of history which we must trace—the development, or we must rather say the degeneracy, of philosophy. The academies of Plato and Aristotle were followed by the academy of Zeno,[1] founded in 311 B.C. and called from its place of meeting the Stoic school. The difference between stoicism and classical Greek philosophy may be roughly described by saying that whereas the Platonic and Aristotelian ways were so utterly conditioned by *theoria* that they could only be called philosophies, Stoicism, and its rival Epicureanism,[2] were sufficiently individualistic, moralistic, and intellectually " soft " to be mistaken by the unwary for

[1] Zeno's reputed dates are 350–253 B.C.

[2] The academy of Epicurus was founded in Athens in 306 B.C.

37

religions. Classical Greek thought proceeded from the assumption that a man could only find his salvation (that is, reality) by the way of abstract thought. Stoicism pursued, not the thing in itself, but *duty* ; Epicureanism, *happiness*. The key-words of Stoicism are the Greek for *self-sufficiency*[1] and *self-mastery*[2]; that of Epicureanism the Greek for "*untroubledness*".[3] It was Stoicism which took hold on the heart of Rome. That a man should need nothing from the world, and should avoid any concession to its blandishments—these were the marks of Stoic greatness, and these were the qualities of the Roman "gentleman", summed up in the untranslatable Latin word *gravitas*. It will be easily seen how such a moral theory, combining a large indifference to the problem of evil with a strict and high-minded personal code would appeal clamorously to those amateur puritans who were the backbone of the Roman patriciate, and equally easily how this argument could pass to the familiar doctrine of the damnation of matter which is the core of the Gnostic curse.

Rome, the comfortless cradle of Christianity, left the contemplation of things to the Athenian highbrows, but Stoicism it took for its own. Its purest incarnations are in the best of the Romans, Cato[4] and Marcus Aurelius[5]; and this stoicism is one of the protagonists in the drama which is now almost ready to begin.[6]

[1] αὐτάρκεια.   [2] ἐγκράτεια.   [3] ἀταραξία.   [4] 234–149 B.C.
[5] b. A.D. 121, *princeps*, 161, d. 180.

[6] Stoicism was, it may be added, neither the only nor even the normal religious philosophy of the Roman population. But it is that which is most relevant to this study because it is in it that the native ideal of Rome is best realised. It will not be difficult to see why, for example, the Sun-worship, which was Christianity's chief competitor in the mind of Constantine, has less bearing on the point we are making here.

But thirdly we must mention something that had happened to music. We have already sufficiently emphasised the connection between music and primitive ecstasy, its development and discipline in Jewish religious worship, and the scrutiny to which it was subjected by the two best minds in classical Greece. What we now have to observe is that under the Roman dispensation music increases considerably in its connotations of " amusement ", and decreases in intrinsic dignity. In classical Greece music was always to be heard at those religious observances which included drama and festive games. That excess in its use was already more than a theoretic danger is sufficiently indicated in what we have quoted from Plato. Since the disciplines of Plato and Aristotle never found their way far beyond the walls of the schools, it may be expected that with the advance of " civilisation " music made its power more widely felt, and as the public religion of Rome became more and more formal, not to say secular, the intellectual and spiritual restraints on public music which were implicitly accepted (if not observed) in the days of Euripides were relaxed, and, in later Roman times, openly set aside. This left the public with a music which appealed to the emotions without carrying with it any exalted connotation whatever, and without manifesting or demanding any of the discipline which in the older view was music's first need. The impression we gain from the early Fathers, from whom we shall shortly be quoting, is that the music of the Roman games was neither religious nor scientific, neither spiritually nor technically admirable.

And not only was music gathering to itself associa-

tions with the frivolous aspects of public life, but the
status of the musician in Roman society was notably
low.   When Greece was absorbed, the absorption was,
of course, only political.   But none the less, the Greek
territory was occupied territory, and the Greek genius
therefore sternly subordinated to Roman needs and
ideals.   Stoicism according to the Romans could not
allow art a high place in its moral hierarchy ; whether
the reason for this was conscious or unconscious in
the Roman mind, it is that the Stoic ideal of " self-
sufficiency " is fatal to the artist.   It was natural,
therefore, that even poets and philosophers often
enjoyed only the status of " freedmen " in the Roman
empire, and that *a fortiori* the musicians, whose art
was at best only ancillary to drama or sport, and at
worst a mere idle amusement, should be consigned
to the lower regions of serfdom.[1]   This does not
mean, of course, that they were chained and branded,
but that they were not thought in virtue of their office
to qualify for that measure of civil right which the
Romans took so seriously.

The purpose of this section has been to indicate the
movement of Greek thought and the temper of Roman
society ; it is vital for our purposes to see Christian
thought in the light of Greek thought and Christian
action in the context of Roman society.   We can now
proceed to the first stages of the encounter between
music and Christianity.

---

[1] The dancer Xenophon, the most distinguished actor of the Byzantine tragic theatre, having allowed his name to be entered on the
" register of mimes " was deprived by the state of his right to inherit
or to appear as a witness in court, and by the church of baptism,
communion, and extreme unction.   (Wellesz, op. cit. 77).

CHAPTER II

THE FIRST FOUR CENTURIES

A.D. 30–451

The Church and its environment—Church authorities on music—St. Augustine's *De Musica*.

(a) THE CHURCH AND ITS ENVIRONMENT

As soon as the Church was born at Pentecost it was clear that no such uncompromisingly divisive force had ever appeared in the world before. Everything and every man was either for it or against it, not only by the nature of the thing or the choice of the man, but also, and more, by reason of the nature of the Church and its message. What the first apostles said[1] was something which of itself made friend or enemy of its hearer ; the Way (as it was primitively called) involved modes of action and allegiance which men were compelled either to accept or to reject with violence. It was one effect of the supernatural nature of this new phenomenon that neutrality towards it was not impiety or imprudence or sloth, but in addition and beyond all these, *non-sense*. It could not be achieved. Gallio, the personation of lofty indifference, goes down to history not as neutral but as on the enemy's side.

Therefore from the beginning the Church was over against much of its environment. What repented was received and redeemed ; what would not repent was the enemy. It was only a matter of a few years,

---

[1] E.g. in the Acts ii. 14-40 and especially 37 ff.

as we see quite clearly in *The Acts*, before the conflict between the church and its environment resolved itself to a fight on three fronts. We must mention these briefly for the sufficient reason that music was part of the environment.

The Church's first duty was to organise itself in such a way that it could most effectively resist physical persecution. Until the edict of Milan, pronounced under the authority of Constantine in 313, the Faith was an " unlawful religion " in the technical sense, and even though through those three centuries active persecution was not without intermission, persecution was always possible and there were only two periods, both during the third century, when the Church felt itself to be free in all its parts from any kind of hostile demonstration. The struggle for some kind of *establishment* was, therefore, the first front on which the Church fought.

The second battle, waged in a different plane, was that metaphysical struggle between the Christian Faith and that which lay behind persecution, namely the Roman brand of stoicism. The outward battle was fought on the technical issue of offering sacrifice to the genius of the emperor. But this was only the foreground of a more significant battle—Christianity *versus* the genius of Rome. Historians have often remarked that the worst enemies of the Faith were the best of the Roman emperors. This is not true in every case, and the conduct of Nero,[1] Domitian,[2] and Galerius (who was really responsible for the persecution attributed to Diocletian)[3] supports the opposite

---

[1] A.D. 54–68.   [2] A.D. 81–96.
[3] A.D. 295–304.

case. But three of the bloodiest and most extensive campaigns of Rome against the Church were those under Marcus Aurelius at Lyons in 177, under Septimius Severus at Alexandria in 203, and under Decius and Valerian in Carthage in 249–50 and 258–9. Marcus Aurelius was one of the best philosophers Rome ever produced, and one of the best emperors. Septimius Severus and Decius were both conspicuous examples of relatively strong and sane leaders following frivolous predecessors, and Diocletian is another in the same category. Therefore it is not without truth to say that those *principes* who took their country's destiny seriously tended to turn upon the Christians as being their country's most dangerous enemies. The genius of Rome, whose philosophical expressions, as we have seen, had so much in common with stoicism, was incompatible with Christianity. The Church could no more give allegiance to a state than it could burn incense to an emperor. The Christian could no more admit a philosophy of self-sufficiency than he could tolerate the image of the emperor on its altar. And so, while the worst of the emperors persecuted for vanity, the best of them persecuted for an ideal ; and whether the persecution was of the one kind or of the other, the Church met it defiantly and victoriously.

But (thirdly) the Church had to deal with a more insidious enemy than either the sword or the genius of Rome. It had to deal with that perversion which is generically named Gnosticism, and which found its way within the gates of the Church at a very early date. Not to enlarge unduly upon the nature of Gnosticism, we may say here that it is that religious temper which

43

condemns matter, denies that God could have created the world and remained good, denies the humanity of the Redeemer, and makes a very strong point of the mysteriousness of the supreme God, who has to be insulated from the corruption of created matter by a series of superimposed " orders of being ". This perversion had great attractiveness, and its mystery-mongering solemnity and mock-ascetic high-mindedness trapped many unwary Christians who thought they were being reverent and disciplined. All the great heresies of the first four centuries can be traced to this source, and the desperate efforts which churchmen made to cleanse the Church's system of lies and keep the truth pure have been the derision of rationalists and the perplexity of many of the well-meaning during subsequent ages. This battle was waged not so much between Christians and pagans as between Christians and Christians, and the history of Christian doctrine in the time of Athanasius, when it all came to a head in the Christological controversies, has all the elements of high tragedy.

The fight proceeded on all three fronts for four hundred years, and the story of it shows how stern and uncompromising the orthodox Christian of the age felt he had to be concerning his worship of the one God, his acceptance of the authority of Christ alone, and his rejection of heresy.

During these four hundred years, then, the Church was building itself up from an obscure band of enthusiasts to a force which could watch the Roman empire go down with equanimity. This growth was not rapid in its early stages, but it was sure. The early pentecostal enthusiasm gave place gradually, as was inevitable, to ecclesiastical planning and polity ; experience was crystallised in doctrine ; minds were sharpened by controversy, and spirits refined by persecution. In times of peace discipline sagged,[1] and the heat of controversy produced theological oddities. The Fathers of the church wrote voluminously and on every conceivable subject.

(b) MUSIC AND THE EARLY CHURCH[2]

But the subject of music in these writings (with the conspicuous exception of those of Augustine) will not be expected to occupy a very large space. In fact, with the exception just mentioned, all the references to music which can be found in the Fathers fall into three groups, which can be tabulated as follows :

1. Those who provide evidence in their writings for primitive musical use.

2. Those who write in praise of music.

3. Those who protest against musical abuse.

Only Augustine has anything to say about music in its own right.

The first group need not detain us long. The reader will be in no need of evidence that music was

[1] See for example Cyprian's *De Lapsis*, written after the Decian persecution (250) which followed the first long period of peace (211–249) which the church had experienced. In this tract the Bishop writes sorrowfully of the loosening of discipline and the lowering of standards during the " peace ".

[2] On this subject compare Wellesz, *A History of Byzantine Music and Hymnography* (1949), chapter III, which deals with the attitude of the Greek church in some detail. The fact that the quotations given there from Greek authors are in so many cases different from those given here is an indication of the extent of the ground to be covered.

from the earliest times natural to the Christian worshipper. Enough has been said, in any case, in the
preceding chapter to establish this. Here and there,
however, we have a reference to a point of practice
which gives a hint of the way in which music was
employed in early Christian worship. Pliny, writing
in about A.D. 115, tells his *princeps* (Trajan) that he
hears of Christians singing "songs to Christ, addres-
sing him as God ". We would give much to know
what these earliest hymns were ; perhaps the Biblical
passages already mentioned give a clue. References
to antiphonal recitation or singing are found in
Tertullian[1] (160-222[2]). That antiphony was not a
Christian invention is shown by the mention made of
Philo, writing in the first century, of antiphonal
singing among the ascetic sect of the Therapeutae ;
and of course, antiphonal singing of such psalms
as the 136th must have been traditional in Jewish
worship.

Hilary of Poitiers (315-67) has an interesting remark in the introduction to his Commentary on the
Psalms[3] where he distinguishes four techniques of
music in worship—*canticus*, which is unaccompanied
singing, *psalmus*, instrumental playing, *canticus psalmi*,
antiphony in which the instrument leads, and *psalmus
cantici*, antiphony in which the singing voices lead.
Ambrose (333-97) likewise mentions the custom of
antiphonal singing.[4] From these authorities we
gather that antiphony of any of three kinds—between

[1] *De Oratione* 27, *Patrologia Latina* I 1194, *De Anima* 9, *P.L.* II 660.
[2] All dates in this chapter must be regarded as no more than
approximate.
[3] *Prologus in Lib. Psalmorum* 19, *P.L.* IX 244.
[4] *Hexaemeron* III 23, *P.L.* XIV 165.

46

precentor and congregation, between groups, and
between instruments and voices, was the rule in the
early church ; nor is this at all surprising when it is
remembered that all music was received by oral tradition only.[2] But this technique, like so many Christian
institutions, was more than merely the product of
necessity. The principle of public worship conducted upon the lines of Statement and Answer,
this technique being symbolic of the truth that
Christian life is properly seen to be a response to
God's initiating act, is as old as Paul[2]; the same
principle is to be found in the twentieth-century
theology of *Wort* and *Antwort* which we associate
with the name of Karl Barth.

The second group of authorities from this period,
containing those comments which express approval of
music, is larger. The most fruitful sources for such
comments are, of course, commentaries on the Psalms ;
most of the Fathers undertook this exercise, using for
the most part the technique of allegory for the purpose
of interpretation. Such a method of exposition will
seem naive to the reader who has the heritage of
rational criticism and " spiritual " interpretation, but
in the primitive church it was considered the only
legitimate method. One of its greatest exponents,
and one of the first to attempt to improve on it, was
Origen,[3] who must share with Augustine the honour
of being credited with the most powerful mind of the
Patristic Age. In commenting upon Psalm 150,

[1] See quotation 24, page 236 which shows that in the seventh century
the writing down of music was unknown in the West.

[2] II Corinthians i. 19-22.

[3] A.D. 185–254.

47

Origen allegorises the various musical instruments there mentioned, comparing the harp with the sensitive soul waiting for the Word of God to play on it, the timbrel with moral discipline, and so on. A comment on Jeremiah similarly states that the trumpet in Scripture is always the symbol of the fortifying power of spiritual strength.[1]

These comments of Origen are by no means so superficial as the reader might at first think. They indicate at any rate two things, of which the first is his acceptance of the power of music for good and the propriety of comparing musical instruments with impulses to virtue. But further than this, his identification of the "timbrel", for which the Latin is *tympanum*, with the character of moral rectitude and spiritual soundness becomes very interesting when it is compared with what was said on page oo about the significance of the percussive instruments in the music of primitive peoples. We may well see in Origen, who was more African than Greek, a direct development along spiritual lines of the same principle.

Other allegorists in this manner are Eusebius, who adopts the same technique in a psalm-commentary,[2] and Basil of Caesarea, who claims with more ingenuity than cogency that the only truly spiritual instrument is the "psaltery", in as much as it produces its sounds not from its lower but from its upper parts.[3]

Such comments as these indicate an *a priori* approval of music, but other passages in the Fathers take us

[1] Quotations 1 and 2, page 224.

[2] Quotation 5, page 226.

[3] Quotation 9, page 228.

further by giving the grounds of the approval. Basil writes generously of the persuasive effects of music, adding what seems a somewhat sardonic comment to the effect that music helps the worshipper to swallow Christian teaching much as sugar helps a patient to swallow medicine.[1] In another place the same author explicitly enjoins the practice of psalmody on his people under threat of expulsion.[2] Athanasius writes in more than one place of the value of psalmody for private devotion.[3] Gregory of Nyssa, who, like Basil, was a Greek-speaking and Greek-thinking Christian, speaks of the virtuous life as " the authentic and true music ",[4] thus echoing the ancient doctrine of *harmonia* which distinguished early Greek thinking on the subject.[5] Eusebius, commenting on Psalm 92,[6] says that music is symbolic of the Christians' deliverance from the Mosaic law—a strange and obscure statement which reads rather like an arbitrary combination of the concept of Christian freedom with that of the goodness of music ; such combinations without coherence abound in the writings of those Fathers who were not always alive to the dangers of allegory. Ambrose testifies to the excellence of music in the words " The man who speaks a hymn of praise speaks spiritually and with a pure heart ",[7] and in another place[8] confesses himself astonished that any man can

[1] Quotation 8, page 228.
[2] Quotation 7, page 227.
[3] *De Virginitate* 20. P.G. XXVIII 275.
[4] *Originalis et vera musica.*
[5] In *Psalmos* III. P.G. XLIV 442.
[6] Quotation 5, page 226.
[7] Quotation 11, page 229.
[8] Quotation 12, page 230.

D

prefer the secular music of instruments to the pure music of hymnody. The most interesting of Ambrose's testimonies, however, is where he says in a psalm-commentary that " The singing of praise is the very bond of unity ",[1] meaning not only that music disciplines the individual mind, but also that congregational singing is a communal exercise of the highest value in realising that supernatural unity which is a distinguishing mark of the Church but which worldly distractions make so difficult of achievement.

Thus the Fathers praise music, first as being so constantly used and written of in Scripture, second as proceeding from the " harmony " of the universe, and third as conducing to proper spiritual discipline. But the same Fathers are not slow to recognise, as Plato did, that music is powerful for evil as well as for good. Lactantius, writing in the fourth century, cautions his reader against " perverting to evil ends that which is given us for the apprehension of divine teaching ",[2] and Basil in *De Legendis Libris Gentilium* offers a similar caution. The most passionate voice, however, is that of John Chrysostom, who feels bound to warn Christians in season and out of season against the pernicious influence of secular music. Almost all his denunciations refer to the music of the pagan theatre, and his observations read like so many paragraphs out of the celebrated *Histriomastix* (1633) of the puritan Prynne. He regards the music of these entertainments as symbolic of everything that is lewd and degrading. " It is," he says[3], " at the root of

[1] Quotation 10, page 229.
[2] Quotation 3, page 225.
[3] *De Leg. Libr. Gent.* 5-7. *P.G.* XXXI 578 ff.

acts of violence and dishonour, wars and daily deaths ;
life for those addicted to these things is dishonourable,
amusements become less and less desirable, and everything at home is turned upside down ".[1]   A glance at
the quotations from his writings given in the Appendix
will make clear not only the strength of his preoccupation but also the variety of its contexts.   He lost
no opportunity of warning his reader against pagan
music.   He was writing, of course, towards the end
of the fourth century, when the Roman empire was
within a decade or two of its final dissolution; its
public life had lost all its dignity and its constitution
all its security ;   the public festivities exhibited every
symptom of incurable decay in civic honour.   What is
interesting about these denunciations by Chrysostom
is the fact that he sees the focus of all this degeneracy
in music, and ascribes to music a monstrous power
both of reflecting and of acting upon a whole
civilisation.

The use of musical instruments in church was a
matter for frequent debate and disagreement.   The
Fathers found themselves obliged on the one hand to
comment upon the musical references in Scripture,
and therefore, in the manner of Origen, to hold up
instruments of music as vehicles for virtue and spiritual
grace in their commentaries.   On the other hand,
the use of instruments was so closely associated with
those theatrical performances upon which Chrysostom
was so severe that as a matter of expediency most of
the Fathers tended to be cautious in advocating them
for use in church.   The Eastern or Greek-speaking
Fathers found it perhaps easier to be happy about

[1] In S. Matt. xxi. 33.   *P.G.* VII 645.   See Quotations 13 to 18, p. 230f.

musical instruments than those, like Ambrose, whose background was Western. We find Basil[1], for example, expressing warm approval of music but doubt about the use of instruments. Ambrose[2] seems to go further and to prefer unaccompanied singing in church, although he is happy to draw a moral from the instruments he finds in Scripture[3].

In all the patristic denunciations of what Ambrose called the " melodies of damnation "[4] we see a striking agreement in regarding the " flute " as the most pernicious of musical instruments, and as focussing the evil of pagan music just as the music focussed the evil of the society it entertained. To introduce a flute into church would have had the effect on the fourth-century Christian conscience which would be produced on our own by the introduction of a dance-band into Westminster Abbey. This is not so surprising as it might seem if it be remembered that the instrument conventionally translated " flute "[5] is really a single-reed instrument, of which the two most familiar modern examples are the clarinet (the most emotive of all orchestral instruments, not excluding the violin), and the saxophone.[6]

But of all the authorities on church music in this period none is profounder than Augustine. His *De Musica*, which is a philosophical treatise, demands separate treatment, but we must refer here to a

---

[1] Cf. Basil, Homily IV in *Hexaemeron* 1. *P.G.* XXIX 81.

[2] Quotation 10, page 229.

[3] Quotation 12, page 230.

[4] *mortiferi cantus.*

[5] αὐλος.

[6] For further references, compare Wellesz, op. cit., pp. 68 ff.

passage in the *Confessions* which will serve not only as a
support for the evidence we have already gathered but
as an introduction to our study of *De Musica*. In this
passage[1] we find in effect a summary of all patristic
thought on church-music. The *Confessions* give us, of
course, not Augustine the theologian, the administra-
tor, or the debater but Augustine on his knees before
God. To read them is to overhear a man at his
prayers. The man we overhear is one who had in his
youth combined an irresponsible avidity for life's
pleasures with a degenerate and Gnostical intellectualism which regarded all created matter as negligible
and all responsible moral teaching as irrelevant[2] ; con-
verted to Christianity, he did not show that fanaticism
or bitterness which might have overtaken, by way of
reaction, a soul of less stature. There is not a page
in the *Confessions* which does not contain both penitence
for sin and also praise to God for what He had made
and done. Augustine's Christian faith is no less full-
blooded and joyful than was his paganism. And so
we read in the passage to which we now refer that
Augustine loved music passionately, that he knows its
power for good and its dangers ; he confesses that he
has himself been distracted by the beauty of the music
from the matter which was being sung, and that this
is falling into error, and yet he will have no excessive puritanism. True to his nature he criticises
Athanasius for what he thinks an over-severe attitude
towards music in church. He treats of church music
with the broad balance and sympathy which he extends

[1] Quotations 20 to 22, pages 233ff.

[2] The precise name for the heresy to which Augustine subscribed is
Manicheism.

to every other subject with which he deals in his greatest work of letters.[1]

To these utterances of the Fathers we should add here the most important of the early ecclesiastical edicts against pagan music. These, be it observed, are not regulations about church music but instructions to Christians to avoid the *musica perniciosa* of the pagan Roman world. The Council of Laodicea (360)[2] denounced those who behave in an improper and frivolous way at Christian festive occasions, and forbade the clergy to remain at a wedding-feast after the actors had appeared. The Council thus formed into a public edict the conviction which found its spiritual expression in Chrysostom.

The other council which issued influential edicts upon music falls outside the period with which this chapter deals but may be mentioned here. Public shows and theatrical performances are anathematised in four canons of the Council *in Trullo* (692),[3] which "marks the climax of resistance against the maintenance of celebrations rooted in pagan customs and rites."

A remarkable parallel to the Christian denunciations of theatrical music is to be found in the edict of Julian the Apostate,[5] quoted at Quotation 19 (page 232) which with a few verbal alterations could have come straight from a Christian source. The use by the

[1] For a more conventionally-expressed approval of music in Augustine' compare *Enarratio in Ps.* 26 (27), *P.L.* XXXVI 199.

[2] J-B Pitra, *Iuris Eccl. Graec. Monumenta* i. 502.

[3] See the twelfth-century comments on this council by Balsamon of Byzantium, *P.G.* CXXXVII 730.

[4] Wellesz, op. cit., pp. 73 ff.

[5] *princeps* A.D. 361–3.

Arians of hymns as a means of propaganda when the Arian controversy was at its height in the fourth century shows that on the question whether music could influence men's minds orthodox and unorthodox were at one.[1]

Thus far, then, we may summarise the Patristic church on church music by saying that its writings and decisions show a keen awareness of the power of music and a desire to guard Christians against music that will damage their faith. If in many places the Fathers show their expertness in theology better than their knowledge of musical principles, and if they seem to lean too heavily on the authority of Plato's moralism, this is only to be expected from those who had to apply principles supernaturally revealed to a science already naturally established. Their advice to the early Church, however shaky its principles, was nothing but excellent in its effect.

(c) THE "DE MUSICA" OF ST. AUGUSTINE[2]

St. Augustine's treatise on music is the single example in all history of independent and original theoretical thinking by a theologian upon music. Our treatment of it, though necessarily sketchy, will be fuller, and will have to contain more technical language, than that which we have given to the other Fathers. The relevance of this section will not fully appear until we come to deal with the nineteenth century, and the reader who is impatient of the

---

[1] See, e.g., Millar Patrick, *The Story of the Church's Song* (1928) p. 31.

[2] This work is translated in part and introduced by W. F. Jackson Knight in "St. Augustine's *De Musica*" published (1949) by the Orthological Institute. This book appeared after the present work had gone to press.

technicalities involved in it can, if he is prepared to accept our word for the argument, pick up our general conclusion on the last pages of the section.

Other theologians have written on music, especially in the Middle Ages, when the kind of learning which was required for the purpose was virtually confined to the monastic houses ; but their work was entirely derivative, and it went no further than combining a grammar of musical theory with a few well-worn moralistic comments taken directly from the pages of Plato. More modern theologians, have, of course, often had opinions to ventilate on the subject of music, but their remarks are in the same class as the patristic comments with which we have just been dealing.

What distinguishes Augustine's work is that it is an application of Christian theology, not to the use of music in church, but to the science of music itself ; the originality of its thought occurs precisely where Augustine combines his musical and his theological learning. The result is so startling that a few pages devoted to it will certainly not be grudged by the reader.

It had better be admitted first of all that for Augustine in this context " music " means something more fundamental and generic than the term means in ordinary modern speech. Its connotation throughout this work is the art of significantly using *sounds* as opposed to words, and what he says applies equally to poetry and to music in the normal sense. But he is not dealing with a topic outside the purview of the musician, nor with a collateral species of art ; he is dealing with that which is common to all those arts which use sounds as the basis of their expression.

He says enough in the course of his essay, however, to make it clear that the principles he is enunciating can be most clearly seen in that art which uses sounds absolutely and which dispenses with words.

De Musica is written in six books, of which it is only the sixth which need engage our attention. The first five books are, as he explains at the beginning of the sixth, of a merely preparatory nature, written so that the import of the sixth can be made clear to those who have no special training. They deal with the principles of prosody, expounding the principles which lie behind the laws determining the use of short and long syllables in Latin verse. These principles he traces back to the quality of *numerositas*, and we are embarrassed at the outset by the fact that this word and its cognate *numeri*, which we shall continually be meeting, are strictly untranslatable. Music, he says, is the *ars bene modulandi* (the art of the well-ordered), and the quality of that which is *bene modulatus* is *numerositas*. The choice of this word indicates that Augustine accepts the connection which the Greeks established between music and mathematics ; but he accepts it (as we may also accept it) not in the sense that music, like mathematics, is basically impersonal and unemotive (which is obviously wrong), but that both music and mathematics are exact forms of expression, matters of delicate adjustment, derived from precise knowledge.

Numerositas is, moreover, a quality of the whole universe, and music in exhibiting it shows itself to be in direct touch with ultimate reality and to be therefore a means of mediating that reality to the hearer. In this conception Augustine is still following closely the teaching which the school of Pythagoras had coined nearly a thousand years before. *Numerositas* is indeed very nearly a Latin translation of the Greek *harmonia*. This quality is diversified in the aesthetic level in certain movements which he calls *numeri*,— movements, as we shall see, which establish the faculty of apprehending music ; they are found both in the music and in the hearer. If this explanation is at all adequate, we now ask the reader's permission to leave the word untranslated in the text. Augustine's thought can only be properly followed in the original language, and to translate this key-word would be to mislead the reader far more seriously than to leave it as it stands.

The sixth book of *De Musica* opens with an apology for the lengthy treatment of prosody which has gone before. Augustine says that his purpose in the work is frankly to provide a gradual passage from devotion to art to devotion to God. He assumes that the properties of verse are well known to most people, but that the properties of abstract music are not so well known, and that he can reach his goal best by starting along a familiar road. But the transition from the study of prosody to the study of " music " is, as the superscription to Book VI declares, the transition from " the study of the mutable *numeri* which are in earthly things to the immutable *numeri* which are the property of immutable truth." Music is more like immutable truth than poetry, in as much as it is less bound up with matter and with created things. Augustine's declared purpose is.

" to separate growing man, or men of any age, not violently but by degrees, from the carnal senses and carnal letters, to which it is so difficult for them not to be attached. Reason must lead them to attach themselves in love and without the interference of nature to the unchanging truth of the one God and Lord of all things who presides over human minds."[1]

The previous books are to be regarded as " part of the journey, not the end of the journey " and Augustine remains impatient of " the mob of clamorous tongues that issues from the schools and takes low and frivolous pleasure in human adulation ". Such people cannot follow him into the sixth book. In fact, he says, the one necessity for those who embark on it is " Christian nourishment ".[2]

" If any reader, through the infirmity of his step or the strangeness of the journey, is unable to follow by this way, nor has the wings of piety so that he can fly past these earlier discussions and forget them, he should not devote himself to business for which he is not equipped ; let him strengthen his wings with the nourishment of the precepts of healthy religion which he will find in the nest of the Christian Faith, and he will then rise on those wings above the dust and toil of the journey, disregarding the tortuousness of the road in his burning love of the Country to which he is going. I write this for those who have given themselves up to secular letters and become involved in grievous errors, wasting good faculties on trifles in ignorance of the pure bliss which is there."[3]

[1] *De Musica, ad init.*
[2] *Ib.*
[3] *Ib.*

Augustine's purpose is to make sense of musical knowledge for the Christian, and he is not at all shocked at the proposition that it will be nonsense to any but a Christian.

In the second chapter he introduces the *numeri* of music, as being the intermediaries between music and pure mathematics. He begins by quoting the first line of the most famous hymn in the church of his day,

Deus Creator omnium

and asking whether its distinctive quality as a piece of verse, to which its rhythm and metre contribute, is a quality in the words, in the hearer, in the sound, or in the speaker. In the ensuing discussion he demonstrates that all these factors enter into any proper analysis of verse or music, and he establishes the existence of five catagories of *numeri*, as follows (here we must lapse into Latin) :

1. *Genus numerorum in ipso sono*—(*numeri* in the sound). This is present, for example, when a sound is uttered in a place where there is no hearer.

2. *Genus numerorum in sensu audientis* (in the hearer), which distinguishes (*a*) one foot from another, as iambus from tribrach, regardless of the speed of utterance, and (*b*) good from imperfect sound. This second category is dependent on the former, but not the former on it.

3.[1] *Genus numerorum in ipso actu pronuntiantis* (in the act of the speaker). This provides for the fact that it is possible to experience the *numerositas* without actual sound being made or received. But this involves the use of memory, therefore he adds

[1] Chapters 3 and 4.

4. *Genus numerorum in ipsa memoria* (in the memory), which can exist independently of the other three *genera* so far mentioned. Finally, falling outside and in a sense embracing the classification which the first four comprise, is

5. *Genus numerorum in ipso naturali iudicio sentiendi* (in the natural judgment). This is the mode of *numeri* which enables a man to distinguish a rhythmical fault, to judge perfection or imperfection in a piece of music or verse. It is the only category which extends its boundaries towards the moral sphere, and is to be distinguished from category (2) as moral judgment is distinguished from technical judgment.

Augustine then proceeds to discuss which is the most important of the categories. Proceeding on the assumption that the soul is superior to the body, and that it is through spiritual channels alone that the Truth can be apprehended (since " matter is lower than its maker "), he place the fifth category, its name now shortened to *iudiciales*, in the first place. The others follow in this order of logical prirority—

> *Progressores* (category 2 above)
> *Occursores* (3)
> *Recordabiles* (4)
> *Sonantes* (1)

The *iudiciales* (5), he says, are alone " absolute " (*immortales*), and he illustrates this statement by the following example. Suppose a rhythm of iambic form (a crotchet followed by a minim) to be uttered where the musical beats are measured in units not of seconds but of days or years. This rhythm could not be detected in any of the four lower categories because

the *numeri in sensu*, of which all the four lower categories are examples, are derivative in nature, whereas
the *iudiciales* are absolute. Put in another way it
amounts to this : although an iambic rhythm in which
the units of length fall outside certain narrowly defined
limits is not detectable by sense, nevertheless if it
were so detectable and there were a fault in it, the
iudiciales would detect that fault and could criticise
it. The *iudiciales*, that is, are purely " theoretical "
(in the Greek sense) and, being in no way dependent
on *consuetudo* (human convention, which is the
limitation of the inferior categories) are the chief
among the *numeri*.

This category of *numeri* is thus established as the
only basis for a faculty of criticism. This is the
subject of Chapters IX and X, which contain matter
of the greatest importance. Here Augustine introduces a new conception—*aequalitas* (symmetry),
which is the property appreciated by the mind in a
piece of music possessing *numerositas*. Music (or
any other form of art : Augustine takes an analogy
from architecture) possessing *numerositas* exhibits
aequalitas to the observer ; and it is from the presence
of this " symmetry " that the characteristic pleasure
attendant on the contemplation of a work of art
originates.

And here lies the root of all the danger in bad
music. For this pleasure is now part of the normal
make-up of man, and he knows the pleasure but not
its origin. What occurs, then, when the symmetry
which gives a man pleasure is not true symmetry,
but only approximate, or what Augustine calls
" imitated " symmetry ? Blunted critical faculties

will not detect the error, and being pleased by a counterfeit symmetry they will become less and less able to appreciate the difference between the counterfeit and the true. Lack of *aequalitas* is the cause of metaphysical badness in music ; *aequalitas* is perfection. And then he adds this :

"Our advice, therefore, is to divert our approval from counterfeit symmetries, where we are unable to discern whether it is counterfeit or true. And yet —in as much as they do imitate the true we cannot deny that in their kind and in their own order they are things of beauty."[1]

Note this most carefully. Augustine has spent half of his book in establishing the principles of perfection, and then he seems to destroy his whole case by saying that the imperfect is after all not to be condemned. That is because he is writing as a Christian theologian and not as a pure philosopher ; it is also because he is writing for ordinary men and not for experts. It is the distinguishing genius of the Christian ethic (as it is expounded at its purest in the Great Sermon in St. Matthew v-vii) that it demands men to be concerned entirely with the struggle for goodness and not at all with the judgment of evil (St. Matthew vii 1). It does not say that evil is not to be recognised as evil, but that the concern of the individual believer in his daily life is to attend to goodness and not to attend to evil. Augustine translates this principle exactly into aesthetics when he says "We need not be caused to stumble by the imperfect ; we need only to delight

[1] 6 : 10 : 28.

in the perfect."[2] Evil in morals and badness in art
are matters of metaphysics and carry their own
judgment.; the practical necessity for the man who
wishes to advance in either goodness or musical
appreciation is to know and to cultivate what is good.

Elaborating this point, Augustine shows that much
evil can be overruled by God for good, taking as an
example the undoubted fact that though adultery is
evil in itself, yet many a good man has been born of
adultery. The same Providence which shapes the
beauty of a work of art can overrule its imperfections.

" In temporal things there is much that seems dis-
orderly and confused, since we judge their order
by comparison with our own standards, ignorant
of the beauty which divine Providence can fashion.
If a man, for example, stands like a statue in some
remote corner of the noblest of buildings, he can
never appreciate the beauty of its construction,
since he is himself a part of the whole. The
soldier in the ranks can never see the whole army.
Similarly in a poem, if the life and work of a syllable
were confined to the time during which it is sound-
ing, no one could be delighted by the beauty and
harmony of the interwoven whole, for that harmony
is composed and fashioned of many single fleeting
moments. So God has ordained men sinful, but
God's order is not sinful. Man has become evil
through his will, and in losing utterly what he could
have held by obeying God's commands ; and man
in his turn is so ordered that, since he himself
refuses to do the bidding of the law, he is compelled

[2] Inferioribus non offendamur; superioribus solum delectamur.

64

by the law. What is in accord with law is just :
what is done justly is not done evilly : for even in
our misdeeds are the good works of God."[1]

Augustine, then, does not advance an unpractical
perfectionism. He only pleads that his reader shall
be constantly discontented with the inferior and
aiming for the higher.

Returning in chapter XII to the eternal *numeri*,
with which the *numeri iudiciales* place us in contact, he
makes the point that the rules of prosody, so elaborately
expounded in the earlier books, can only be regarded
as timeless and immutable. Who, he asks, would at
this time of day think of altering the value of the long
first syllable in the word *Italia* ? Rules of this kind
are simply the expressions of God's own " unchange-
able truth ".

We can, then, despite all these precepts, love what
is imperfect, because we can be content with the
delight of the senses and miss the delight of the in-
tellect. It is fatally easy to be *content* with those
counterfeit " symmetries " which deceive the inferior
numeri in ourselves so long as the *iudiciales* are in
abeyance. Augustine (ch. XIII) enumerates the
particular dangers that lie in the way of the " inferior " categories, and there follows a remarkable
conclusion.

" It is the love of action (sc. as opposed to " contemplation ") that distracts the soul from the Truth,
and the origin of this love is in pride. Pride is the
vice which makes men prefer imitating God to
serving Him. Rightly is it written in Holy

[1] 6 : 11 : 30.

E

Scripture, ' The beginning of pride is rebellion from God ', and ' pride is the beginning of all sin '. Pride could not be better demonstrated than from what stands written there. ' Why is earth and ashes proud ? Because in his life he hath cast away his bowels '.[1] The soul by herself is nothing ; whatever she is is of God. Remaining in her own order she may live in the presence of God Himself in mind and conscience ; and this is her own proper good. The soul swollen with pride goes forth beyond her own order, becomes vain, and so (paradoxical though it appears) becomes less and less. What is this going forth beyond herself but ' casting away her bowels '? That is, to place God far from her, not in space, but in the affections of the mind."[2]

Pride, to Augustine, is a violation of the symmetry of the universe, that " order " which God has made.[3] It is pride which makes men want for themselves powers that belong to God, of which the symbolic disobedience of Adam is one example, and the arbitrary meddling with the supernatural rules of *numerositas* is another. What Augustine calls the " love of action " is the direct opposite of that contemplation which to his philosophic predecessors is respect for the thing *in itself*. " Love of action " is the characteristic of the person who will tolerate nothing that he has not himself invented, thought of,

[1] Ecclus x. 9-15.

[2] 6 : 13 : 40.

[3] It may be remarked here that at this climatic point Augustine introduces the word *Ordo* (order), which is one of the basic ideas of his *City of God*. See page 89.

66

modified, or experienced ; who can see nothing as it, regarding everything as given to him for his own use, not as demanding from him the courtesy of an un-selfconscious attention. And this, says Augustine, is at the root of bad art and failure to appreciate the good. The rebellious will can neither seek nor make good music.

The final chapters elaborate these points, and conclude with a reference to the eternal *numerositas* which only the risen soul in the presence of God can experience.

The importance of *De musica* can be summed up as follows :

1. It is the most complete synthesis of music and theology that has ever been achieved. Music to Augustine is primarily a metaphysical phenomenon, but it is also an activity of men and therefore subject to moral judgments. Only a Christian, he says, can hope to deal with the problems which this raises.

2. Being a Christian, he allows full value to the pleasure content of music, and never advises his reader to beware of pleasure as such.

3. Also, being a Christian, he solves the problem of " badness " in music. That imperfection which is the heritage of all created things he tells his reader to tolerate and not to make into an occasion for abandoning his study. That which proceeds from wilful disregard of the laws of symmetry and soundness he roundly denounces as pride and therefore sinful.

4. Above all, Augustine regards music as an activity of the reason, not a matter of feeling and " self-

expression ". It is the *Logos* which is the expression of eternal and immutable things, not the human *logos*, which is tainted with all human failings. Music for him brings the truth down from heaven, and those who regard music as a means of sending thoughts up from the human mind will do well to mark his words.

CHAPTER III

THE MIDDLE AGES[1]

(*First Part*, A.D. 451 *to* 1100)

Ecclesiastical and Secular Politics—Music in the East—
Music in the West.

(*a*) ECCLESIASTICAL AND SECULAR POLITICS

The most important single movement of history in
this period is the widening of the cleavage between
the Eastern and Western halves of the Mediterranean
civilisation. A previous chapter mentioned those
elements in Greek-speaking civilisation which were
not soluble, in the Roman crucible. As the Roman
Empire increasingly suffered from internal degeneration and from pressure from the " barbarians " of the
further East (notably Persia) this cleavage became the
more marked. The critical situation on the Eastern
frontiers caused Constantine to move his headquarters
to Byzantium (Constantinople) in 324, and at the same
period the Arian controversy divided the newly-
freed Christian world sharply between the free thinkers

[1] This chapter and the next are more than usually dependent on the
text-books, and it will be well to recommend to the reader three books
which deal each with one aspect of the subject we are here treating.
Christopher Dawson's *The Making of Europe* (Sheed and Ward, 1939)
is an excellent treatment of the general history of the time ; Reginald
Lane Poole's *Introduction to the History of Medieval Thought and Learning* (S.P.C.K., 1884 and 1920), though an old book, is a beautifully-
presented and scholarly account of theological developments ; and
Gustav Reese's *Music in the Middle Ages* (Dent, 1941) is a highly technical modern work, as trustworthy on its subject as it is exhaustive.

of the East and the orthodox conservatives of the West. The fall of Rome in 410 left Byzantium as the effective capital of the political world and the axis of power in the Mediterranean empire was for the following centuries not, as in the fourth, between one Caesar at Byzantium and another (slightly inferior) at Rome, but between the head of the State in Byzantium and the head of the Church in Rome.

This had the strange consequence what while Rome was politically a city whose native people were under the heel of conquering foreigners and therefore scarcely significant in the Mediterranean empire, the Christian city of Rome emerged into great importance and became within a century the one power with which Byzantium had seriously to reckon. After the conversion of the mighty conqueror Clovis to Christianity in 493 Rome became a frankly Christian capital. During the next few decades Justinian, the native Roman emperor in Byzantium (483–565), found his autocratic dreams seriously threatened by the existence of the Roman bishop, and whether he had to oppose one bishop or buy off another, there was no ignoring the Pope in any concern of public importance. In Rome the very invasion which crushed the power of the Caesars gave the Church its opportunity of power. The catastrophe which let the barbarians in let the Christians out.

This meant not only the new political significance of the Pope (which in later centuries was to be the pivot of European history) but also new opportunities for missionary work, which the Church grasped eagerly. The conversion of Clovis opened a direct line of communication between Rome and the scattered Christian communities of Gaul, and for a time the Faith spread quickly. In the meantime a Frenchman named Patrick had brought Christianity to the Scots (who lived at that time in Ireland) and thus (A.D. 432) a tradition of contemplative Christianity was started there which has never been eradicated from the native Irish character. In the next century (563), Columba established the northern home of Christian culture at Iona, whence the conversion of Scotland was pressed forward, and in 597 Augustine was sent by Gregory the Great to carry out an historic mission to England.

Now it was characteristic of the temper of these centuries of expansion that the Christian settlements tended to take the form not of isolated churches but of monasteries. The first monasteries in Christendom were the foundations of heretical ascetics (the Montanists), and the first orthodox monasteries, founded in the early fourth century in Africa and Asia minor, were predominantly retreats from either the physical dangers or the moral temptations of the world. The early medieval communities, though retaining something of the fort-like character of the earlier monasteries, were larger and perhaps more genial foundations ; their purpose was to provide not so much an asylum for refugees or a forcing-house for Christian athletes as normal hospitality in which the Faith might grow most happily. They became, in a primitive way, outward-looking and inclusive rather than intense and exclusive. They became centres of learning as well as of Christian teaching, and in them were the sources of the whole of the medieval Christian culture and the channels by which it was transmitted.

So well was this establishment carried out that when the tide flowed once again against the Church in the Dark Ages and the monasteries became once more refuges from the barbarian hordes, the Church was never submerged. When France was in confusion, Ireland held the fort, and when Ireland was overrun, France carried on the good work.

This expansive movement was, unfortunately but not unnaturally, accompanied by a sharp decline in theological consciousness. The age of the codification of doctrine seems to close abruptly with the Council of Chalcedon (451). Controversy did not cease, nor did heresy die. Chalcedon was not a victory so much as a milestone. But all the essentials of Christian doctrine had been established by minds sharpened by controversy, and the answers of the great Councils of the Fourth and Fifth centuries were the answers not only to the questions which had been asked already but also to those which were going to be asked during the next thousand years.

But if the minds of Christians had turned away from theological statements, they turned very naturally towards classical learning and the broader humanities of culture. The problem of the Church in a friendly world was, for its medieval administrators, focused in the problem of what the Church was to do with the letters and philosophy of Greece and Rome, both classical and contemporary. Nothing could have been more salutary than this humane enrichment of dogmatic Christianity, so long as Christians were men of the spirit " naturally theological ", that is, men who, scarcely making a conscious effort, referred the findings of pagan culture to the precepts of their Faith.

The Christian *literati* of the fourth century, like those of the thirteenth, were men of this order. Lactantius, Ambrose, and Hilary of Poitiers, all of whom appeared in our last chapter, are the first fruits of Christian classical culture.

But when the flood of theology gradually ebbed, and Christians could no longer be relied on to keep their appreciation of pagan humanities within the bounds of Christian piety, there arose a new spiritual crisis which the great Roman bishop, Gregory the Great (590–604), took measures to resolve. Gregory may easily be misunderstood as an enemy of culture from his edicts against the excessive attention being paid to classical learning. But his object was to substitute a Christian culture for a heathen culture, even an efficient Christian culture for a poor and emasculated heathen culture, and to restrict the inflow of pagan thought into minds insufficient in theological soundness to deal with its excess. Gregory's activities in the *schola cantorum* (which if he did not actually found, he certainly vitalised) show him a man of austerity and a lover of the unpretentious, but in no way an enemy of the beautiful or the true. If he saw better than his contemporaries that the " full " and " rich " life is the dangerous life for the Christian we have no evidence that he positively demanded of the Christian the exercise of cowardice. It is discretion that is excellently displayed in all his work on church music and on that humane culture of which music was by now an acknowledged part.

But of course the decline of classical learning which followed Gregory did not bring with it any theological revival. With the exceptions perhaps of Boethius and John Scotus Erigena there is scarcely a sign of sound and constructive theological thinking between Augustine, and Anselm (1033–1109). And so Europe entered on a period of almost unrelieved barrenness. The light of the Faith was not extinguished nor were the monasteries overwhelmed ; but ignorance dimmed the light and false teaching poisoned the monasteries. And if the drying up of classical learning freed men's minds for scholastic theology, it withdrew from them that philosophical athleticism which had been the fourth century's chief weapon against falsehood. The classical revival under Charles the Great (Emperor of the Holy Roman Empire 800–814) produced a temporary access of learning ; but the revival was too short-lived, too far dependent on the support of a powerful and only doubtfully constitutional monarch, to amount to more than the drifting into Western Christendom of a few scattered ideas and verses from the classics. The fact that the best philosopher of the period, John Scotus Erigena (c. 815–880) had his Plato from a debased edition of the *Timaeus,* and had no Aristotle at all, indicated well enough the degeneracy of scholarship which characterises even this period of comparative enlightenment. None the less the age of Charles the Great saw a " renaissance " bright enough to deepen the darkness of the period following, an age of oppression, wandering, and superstition, an age in which the leaders of the Church tried to establish a temporal empire relying on forged documents and crude force while they allowed the Christian Truth to be engulfed in a quicksand of perversions and absurdities of such delirious picturesqueness as not even the Patristic Age had ever witnessed.

And yet during the century following Charlemagne one principle was established which the succeeding centuries regarded as a settled axiom. This was the principle that the Church was the arbiter of all things. It is during the Middle Ages, as distinct from both the Patristic and the post-Reformation eras, that one can speak of " The Church " meaning a unified authority which if not universally accepted even by Christians was at any rate limited geographically rather than doctrinally. However corrupt, misguided, oppressive and even openly impious " The Church " was, it was still " The Church ". An unconscious Platonic insight saw within the external accidents of the Church a " form " or " idea " of a transcendent Church which was the bearer of authority. This principle shows itself in the monopoly which the Church held, by common consent, of scholarship and culture, in the political ambitions of Hildebrand,[1] in the assumption in law of a transcendent Good to which all law was subject, and finally and most impressively in the mighty theological system of St. Thomas Aquinas, which made theology " queen of the sciences ". Further effects of this we shall meet in the next chapter ; its relevance here is that already what was said about music, as about everything else, was said by the Church.

The mighty exception to the universality of the Church, the permanent obstacle to the realisation of the catholic dreams of Hildebrand, was the Eastern Schism. The cleavage between East and West was

[1] Pope Gregory VII, 1073–85.

not a single historical event, but a condition of things which gradually became more and more apparent and inescapable. Occasions for friction became more frequent as the years advanced towards the millennium. The final occasion, the secession of 1054 which remains unresolved to this day, was the fifth occasion when the Eastern Church went out of communion with the West. The fourth had been the Iconoclastic controversy, which kept the two halves of the Church out of communion from 726 to 787 and again from 815 to 843, a total of almost a hundred years. The fact was that whether the East was or was not officially in communion with the West, its religion and culture followed a course totally different, and yet the boundary between East and West was always a spiritual one across which cultural communications could to some extent be maintained. This is why the music of the Byzantine church was able to develop itself comparatively freely, and why despite the distinction between Byzantine music and Gregorian music, the influence of East upon West was by no means negligible as the ages passed.

Moreover, if East was sundered from West finally by a credal clause, and if traditionally the East and West could not lie down in peace together, the East regarding itself as the birthplace of the Faith and the West as its proper and permanent home, none the less the common threat of Islam, from the seventh century onwards, tended to throw East and West together. This was by no means a case of organic and conscious union against a common foe, but two great moments of history show the effect of Islam as throwing the East on the mercy of the West in spite of itself and in defiance of the traditional schism.

The first occasion was the Iconoclastic controversy, whose relevance will be seen in a moment. This controversy was centred on the question whether sensual (in particular, visual) aid to worship was permitted to Christians. Its rather odd origin may be briefly stated thus, that the emperor Leo III (717–740), failing signally in his efforts forcibly to convert the Jews and the Moslems, found himself impressed by the religious tenacity of his enemies ; this he attributed not without justice, to that fanatical opposition to the use of " images " or visual aids to worship which characterised Islam and which derives from the prohibition expressed in the second commandment of *Exodus* XX. Without concerning himself to find out the historical and theological origins and development of the doctrine, he proclaimed a religious policy of " image-destruction " or *Iconoclasm* throughout the empire. The Western half of Christendom was not impressed by this announcement, and there followed the protracted controversy to which we have referred. During that controversy we find what perhaps we should not have expected, that the East took the puritan line in opposition to the West. Although there was official schism, none the less the controversy made the two halves of the empire conscious of one another, and even the acrimonious interchange of ideas was more fruitful than silence would have been.

The other occasion when in spite of their differences East and West were thrown together was when Byzantium fell finally to the Moslems in 1453, thus releasing a flood of refugees towards the West and fertilising European culture with oriental humanism. To the fateful results of this event we shall attend in their proper place.

(*b*) MUSIC IN THE EAST[1]

We mention this in order to give some sort of explanatory background for what we shall now say about the development of music and musical theorising. For in the two halves of Christendom the activities are quite distinct. We may begin by noting, without much attention to detail, what had been happening in the East.

While the West was entering on a long period of sterility, the inventive tradition of the East persisted, and the culture which produced the philosophy of Leontius (485–543) and the theology of John of Damascus (d. 750) was also producing a new and rich heritage of liturgy and music. The Eastern church developed a notable technique for setting forth the Christian Faith in sacred song. Scholars divide the development of Byzantine music into two distinct periods separated by the Iconoclastic controversy. In the earlier period, from the fourth to the seventh century, Byzantine liturgical music was at its highest in the *Contakion*, a hymn of considerable length whose words were specially composed but founded in Scripture and traditional doctrine. The form is found at its best in the reign of Justinian (527–565) and its most distinguished exponent was one Romanos

[1] The authority on this subject is Dr. Egon Wellesz, to whose chief work in English we referred on page 9. We may refer here to an article by him in English on Byzantine Music in the *Proceedings of the Musical Association* (1932), pp. 1 ff.

(*fl.* 540), whose style is derived from that of the Syrian musician Ephraim (*fl.* 370). The influence of Romanos was continued in the patriarch Sergius (*fl.* 630). In its musical style the Contakion at its best shows restraint and avoidance of the secular idiom. Its music is, indeed, of the very simplest, and there is as yet no system of notation at all.

After the pause which the Iconclastic controversy very naturally caused in musical composition (since music is within the bounds of " aids to worship ") a new form of liturgical music appeared, namely the *Canon*. The literary form of the Canon was somewhat more restricted than that of the Contakion ; it consisted of nine odes,[1] each of which contained normally four strophes, and each ode corresponded fairly closely with one of nine " odes " taken from Scripture.

The Iconoclastic controversy did not, of course, cause a complete breakdown in musical tradition so much as a temporary retarding of it, and in fact the " classics " of this Canon form were composed while the controversy was still in progress. Some early masters of the form were St. Andrew of Crete (650–730), Germanos (645–745) Cosmas of Jerusalem (d. 760) and St. John of Damascus (*fl.* 750) ; later exponents, during the relatively peaceful ninth century when the West had begun to disintegrate, were Theophanes (759–842) and St. Joseph, members of the " School of the Studion ", and the Emperor

[1] These odes were : The Song of Moses (Ex. xv), the Exhortation of Moses (Deut. xxxii), the Canticle of Hannah (I Sam. ii), The Canticle of Habakkuk (Hab. iii), the Canticle of Isaiah (Isa. xxvi), the Canticle of Jonah (Jon. iii), the Song of the Three Children (from the Apocrypha) in two parts, and the Magnificat (Lk. i).

Leo VI (886–917).[1]   During this period a system of
notation developed from the "ecphonetic" method
(which was confined to accents over important syllables
indicating the general direction of the melody)
towards the complete system which was perfected in
the fifteenth century.   But as we shall see, it was in
the West that notational progress was more rapid.

A parallel musical tradition can be seen in the
Armenian church, which was a schismatic body
separated from the Eastern orthodox church on the
issue of Monophysitism in 536.   The hymns of this
church, which until the year 1080 were all in prose,
were gathered into a canon in 1166, and their music
is clearly of the same kind as that of Byzantium.

There is no need to go further into the history of
Byzantine music, which is one of those specialised
studies which the present book can only mention by
references.   The point to be made here is that the
history of Byzantine music is the story of a church
music developing naturally into a form which won the
acceptance of this whole section of the church.   The
only sign of criticism we see in the Eastern church is
the "backwash" of the Iconoclastic controversy.

(*c*) MUSIC IN THE WEST

Criticism as such is hardly more frequent in the
West, but what the monasteries did produce was a
long series of technical works on music, which reflect
the musical developments of the passing centuries.
The foundations of musical studies within the

[1] A glance at any of the standard modern hymnals will show the
reader how much the modern church owes, through the translations
and imitations of John Mason Neale (1818–66) to the literature of the
later Byzantine liturgies.

quadrivium (the standard curriculum of Christian learning, largely established by the influence of Gregory) were in the works of Boethius (c. 480–524), Cassiodorus (485–580) and Isidore of Sevile (570–636).

Boethius was born in Rome and spent his life there as a philosopher and statesman. He was eventually condemned to death by Theodoric on a charge of treason, having by his tenacious orthodoxy been at issue with the Arianism of the emperor. He mediated Greek learning to Rome by translating works of Plato, Aristotle, Pythagoras, and Euclid, and his greatest surviving work was *De Consolatione Philosophiae*. His musical writings were extensive, and they combine the theory of the second-century Alexandrian scientist Ptolemy with the general critical outlook of Plato. He echoes Augustine's appreciation of the element of *similitudo* in music, and looks on music, in the manner of the Greek scientists, as a true link between the phenomenal and eternal worlds. He believed music to be recognizable in three aspects —*musica mundana*, the music of the spheres, or cosmic harmony ; *musica humana*, the harmony of the human soul ; and *musica instrumentis constituta*, music performed. He accepted Plato's dictum that certain modes could be *lascivi* (morally reprehensible), and could induce degeneracy in individuals and in the state. His normal theory of music, indeed, is entirely derived from Plato and not at all from Aristotle ; he gives no sign of understanding the more intimate meaning of Augustine's treatise, though he clearly had read it. But, no doubt because of its simplicity and lack of profundity combined with clear writing and sound wisdom, his treatise had an influence which was denied to Augustine's.

Cassiodorus also was a man of public affairs as well as a philosopher, but he had better success than Boethius, and after a long life in the civil service of the emperors Theodoric and Justinian retired to a monastery and lived to be nearly a hundred. His work on music is as extensive as that of Boethius, but of less importance. His *De Musica* covers the same ground as the work of Boethius, except that it introduces some of the principles of Aristoxenus. Like Boethius and the Platonists he regards music as " a discipline that is dispersed through all the activities of our life ",[1] and he quotes Augustine's definition of music as the *ars bene modulandi*. He is inclined to be more tolerant of musical instruments than the Fathers of the fourth century and in one place uses the psaltery as the symbol of Christ. In a letter to Boethius he shows that he does not altogether accept the Platonic condemnation of certain modes, and is rather inclined to favour the Aristotelian method of assigning to each mode its proper virtue and function.[2]

Isidore, archbishop of Sevile, gives in his *Etymologies* a summary of Cassiodorus, and in his *De Ecclesiasticis Officiis* has some interesting information about the church usages in Spain in his time. Beyond this, however, he has nothing new to contribute.[3]

These then were the musical authorities of the earlier Middle Ages. During and after the Carolingian renaissance there appears a series of scholars whose

[1] *De Musica*, Migne, *P.L.* LXX, 1209 A.
[2] Quotation 24, page 236.
[3] Quotations 25 and 26, page 237.

work corresponds not to any movement of theological thought but to developments in purely musical theory.[1]   Alcuin of York (735–804), one of Charles's earlier spiritual advisers, gives the first mention of the appearance of the oriental " echoi "[2] in the West. Aurelian of Réomé (*fl.* 850) has some observations on melodic formulas.   Hucbald (840–?930) has some important comments on the early *organum*.   Regino of Prüm (d. 915) gives the first of the *tonaria*, which are systematic editions of the antiphons and responses by modes.   Odo of Cluny (d. 942) in his *Dialogus* shows the first systematic use of letters for musical pitches from which the modern nomenclature is derived, and Guido of Arezzo (995–1050) perfected the four-line staff-notation for plainsong.   Notker Labeo (d. 1022) writes on the measurements of organ-pipes, and Berno (d. 1048) hints at certain experiments in the monochord.   Beside these inventive scholars there are those whose work consisted in commentary on earlier authors, such as Rhabanus Maurus (d. 856) and Rémy (Remigius) of Auxerre (*fl.* 890).   It would be churlish in an English author to omit mention of the Venerable Bede's work *Musica Practica*,[3] although we are not able to say that it adds anything to the musical thought or research of earlier scholars, devoting as it does much space to the barren study of the numerological aspects of music.

To the conclusion that the musical scholars of this

[1] The material in this paragraph is a summary of that given in Gustav Reese, op. cit., pp. 127 ff.

[2] For a discussion of the echoi, whose appearance observed by Alcuin is, of course, evidence of Byzantine influence, see Reese, op. cit. pp. 84-90.

[3] Migne, *P.L.* XC 922.

period (800–1100) are scientists rather than theologians there are two important exceptions, Agobard of Lyons (779–847) and John Scotus Erigena (c. 815–880).

Agobard[1] was no great theologian by general standards, but he had as acute a mind and as lively a conscience as any churchman of his age. He was one of the leading ecclesiastical statesmen in the reign of Charles the Great, succeeding in this capacity Alcuin of York. In the Iconoclastic controversy he was a supporter of Charles the Great (that is, he was in favour of the condemnation of " images ") but his opinions on the matter were expressed in terms more calm and logical than those employed by most of his contemporaries. In matters of controversy he showed a combination of liberality and strength of purpose which is exemplified excellently in his comments in *De Correctione Antiphonarii* on musical uses. Here his principles were to reform without unsuitable innovation and to purify without robbing his material of vitality. His reverence for Gregorian austerity and his criticisms of oriental elaboration are brought out in the quotations which we give from this work.[2] These comments of his stand alone in this age as musical criticism, and they indicate the mind of the Church at the time. They do not, of course, bring any fresh material to bear on our subject, but their very presence in this theoretic age is notable.

John Scotus Erigena is the leading theologian of

---

[1] On Agobard, see Lane Poole, op. cit., pp. 34-45, where it will be found that in his dealings with the Jews Agobard deviated notably from his liberal ideal (p. 41).

[2] Quotations 27 and 28, pages 237 ff.

the age.   His theology is distinguished for its vision-
ary inventiveness rather than for its philosophical
solidity.   The line of communication between him
and his acknowledged master, Plato, is long and
tenuous owing to the Gregorian reforms of scholastic
learning, but his mind was a searching one, and his
thinking was on the scale of greatness.   We must
therefore not pass unmentioned his references to
music in the *De Divisione Naturae*,[1] where he makes
much of the connection between music and cosmic
harmony.

With the best will in the world, however, we can
gather no more than this in the way of musical thought
from the theologians of this time.   But what is of
great importance is the development of music which is
reflected in the work of the medieval theorists.   Of
this development we can only here mention the two
most important aspects, namely the growth of plainsong melody and the appearance of *organum*.

The melodic enrichment of plainsong reached its
zenith in the West during the tenth century.   Its
greatest exponent was Hermannus Contractus (Her-
man the Cripple :   1013–1054), whose celebrated
melody *Alma Redemptoris Mater*[2] is a typical example
of plainsong at its best.   The words are a prose
antiphon from the Missal, and they are set to music
which in its use of compound neumes (groups of
notes set to single syllables) follows the sense and
cadence of the words with an expressiveness as precise
as it is moving.   In the whole composition there are
no groups of more than four notes except the very

[1] Migne, *P.L.* CXXII 638.
[2] Quoted in Reese, op. cit. p. 128.

first group of all, on the first syllable of *Alma*, which has thirteen notes. The effect of this is a triumphant flourish followed by restrained richness. (The melody is interesting for two other reasons, which may be noticed in passing. It employs the flattened fourth of the scale, which turns the Lydian mode into the modern major scale, and its opening flourish is obviously the germ from which springs that great family of Genevan psalm-tunes of which *Psalm* 138[1] is probably the best known example). Other examples of " silver-age " plainsong are in the work of Robert the Pious of France (995–1031), Peter Abélard(1079–1142) and Hildegard of Bingen (d. 1179).

Organum, the other musical development to which the theorists attend (notably Hucbald) is, for our purposes, the practice of allowing two voices to sing simultaneously a fifth or a fourth apart. Here are Hucbald's words :

> " Consonance is the judicious and harmonious mixture of two tones, which exists only if two tones, produced from different sources, meet in one joint sound, as happens when a boy's voice and a man's voice sing the same thing, or in that which they commonly call *Organum*.."[2]

In the *Musica Encheiriadis* (which is not now thought, as it formerly was, to be Hucbald's work) *organum* is shown to be capable of certain variations, and it becomes clear that four voices singing in fifths and fourths (that is, parallel fifths) were regarded as

---

[1] *Songs of Praise* (1931) 661 and *Cambridge Carol Book* XLII. Compare the melody from the Bohemian Brethren's *Gesangbuch* of 1566 called *Mit Freuden Zart, Songs of Praise* 214.

[2] *De Marmonica Institutione*, quoted in Reese, op. cit. p. 253.

producing a sound not only pleasing but also natural by the musicians of the tenth century. *Organum* is therefore the first stirring of the harmonic instinct in music, though it cannot be called in any proper sense harmony, still less polyphony, since the " parts " are in no sense independent. But its appearance is clearly connected with two natural facts, namely that the fifth of the scale is the first " overtone " of any fundamental note after its octave, and (which was probably more present to the consciousness of the first exponents of *organum*) that the interval between the ranges of the lower and higher men's voices is roughly a fifth. To this may be added the theory of Dom Anselm Hughes that before *organum* appeared the repetition of a Gregorian melody a fifth higher was not an unknown practice. Clearly this is a development of music of a purely " natural " kind, deriving from the mathematical and practical observation of the asymmetrical division of the octave which was, we can now see, implicit in all musical structures from the time of Aristoxenus onwards.[1] But nobody in the tenth century foresaw what this development was going to lead to in the thirteenth.

Music, then, occupied a place of high honour in the Church of the earlier Middle Ages. All the commentators to whom we have attended, and many others of the same kind, devout Christians, regarded music as an important part of man's religious life. The integral connection between music and the " harmony of the universe " and between music and human morals, re-established by Boethius, is held without question through these centuries. On the other hand,

[1] The whole matter is discussed in Reese, op. cit., pp. 250 ff.

music is still a relatively tractable force, being regarded by all these theorists as a branch of science or mathematics reather than in the modern fashion as an " art ". It is in the next five centuries that music breaks loose from the comfortable bondage in which it remained up to the appearance of the *organum*. To this development, one of the chief anxieties of the church and one of the crowning glories of the later Middle Ages, we must now turn.

CHAPTER IV

THE MIDDLE AGES, SECOND PART

1100–1325

The New Synthesis—Musical Developments—The Attitude of the Church.

(*a*) THE NEW SYNTHESIS

We have been dealing with an age of failure : we now turn to an age of success. The focus of the last chapter was the ninth century ; the focus of this will be the thirteenth. The difference between the two centuries, in some respects so much alike, will soon become clear. It can best be stated in terms of that vision which was, as far as the description can be given to any single event, the beginning of the Middle Ages, the *De Civitate* of Augustine. *De Civitate*, written while Rome was falling before the barbarians, envisaged a mighty and supernatural monism of Church and State ; its subject-matter amounts to a prophecy of a temporal Law which is based on supernatural Grace, a religious society whose piety is its law and whose virility its principle of order.

The Holy Roman Empire of Charles the Great was a recollection of this principle, and its failure is the measure of the incompleteness of the recollection. Similarly the temporal ambitions of Pope Nicholas I (858–867), who strove to capitalise for the Church the political disintegration of Europe, though they proceeded from a genuine Christian desire for the

" tranquillity of order ", were none the less too obviously based on crude force and perversions of historic truth to come to any good effect. But in this century for the first time attempts were made to give play to those forces which made for unity. That the forces were thought to be natural when in Augustine's vision they are supernatural is the reason for the collapse of the attempt ; but the reason was a human one. And even though the synthesis of the ninth century remained only a distorted recollection of Augustine's vision, the succeeding darkness and confusion never wholly obliterated it from the minds of popes and princes. And in exactly the same fashion the theological revival of the ninth century, though it came to no immediate success, did yet display an energy which was recaptured after the historic judgment had fallen sufficiently upon early medieval error.

It is in the thirteenth century that the new synthesis is attempted, and we find in that century a great effort, more enlightened and comprehensive than that of the ninth century to bring all things under a single spiritual authority. That which, in the ninth century, found authority for its practical expression in such chicaneries as the Forged Decretals and the Donation of Constantine[1] was now worked out from the grounds of honour and expediency. It is during these centuries that the battle between synthesis and confusion is fought out, and the final issue of that battle, as everyone knows, was not a victory for synthesis. For despite the high ideal of St. Augustine's *De Civitate*[2]

[1] B. J. Kidd, *Documents Illustrative of the History of the Church*, vol. III (1941), articles 49 and 67.

[2] *De Civitate* Book xix.

synthesis became too closely allied with slavery; freedom was relegated too arbitrarily to the category of the divisive and confusing. Authority, temporal or spiritual, had to depend too much on physical force. The sanctity of the individual, though theologically admitted, was in practice not respected but feared and hunted.

These generalisations may be illustrated by reference to certain familiar events of the later Middle Ages. It is clearly the conclusion to be drawn, for example, from papal policy from Gregory VII (1073–85) to Boniface VIII (1294–1302). Hildebrand (Gregory VII), described by B. J. Kidd not unjustly as " one of the greatest Roman pontiffs and one of the most remarkable men of all time ",[1] sought a European unity which should depend on the Pope and the Prince; but since he regarded temporal power without spiritual regulation as positively evil, the Prince must play *discantus* to the Pope's *cantus*. He did not live to see the full fruit of his policy, and in fact the policy depended too much on the pontiff's startling energy and personal strength of purpose to be safe. Tyrants, even in the spiritual sphere, be they never so benevolent, cannot bequeath their authority. But the principle established itself firmly, and in Innocent III (1198–1216) we see its full flower in the nearest approach the Church ever made to the realisation of Augustine's ideal.

And yet, with Pope and Prince even thus far at one concerning the mission and destiny of Christian civilisation, the story of the Crusades,[2] that long

[1] Kidd, op. cit., art. 89. For Hildebrand's policy see the summary of the *Dictatus Papae* at art. 96, and for his impressively humble attitude to his office, see the letter to Hugh of Cluny, art. 92.

[2] Lagarde, *The Latin Church in the Middle Ages* (1915), pp. 481 ff.

procession of missionary adventures based on force, is
nothing but a record of misguided enterprise and
accumulated failure. The Inquisition,[1] which was
meant to be the safeguard of Christian Truth, became
the focal point of papal infamy. Indulgences,[2]
originally a harmless enough device revived in the
eleventh century in order to allay the anxieties of
people whose relatives died unshriven in the Crusades,
became, by association with a too closely organised
church-system, the blasphemy against which Luther
marched with implacable energy.

That " order " which Augustine had dreamed of,
and of which Gregory VII had more than a superficial
grasp, crumbled in the hands of those who sought to
build it, because they sought to build it in the wrong
materials. It became impatient, inhuman, unpractical
and false, and so it remained unredeemed. The
thirteenth century, with its sharp contrasts of civilisation and confusion, vendetta and pomp, culture and
crusade, is the scene of the greatest drama of European
history before the Reformation.

The theological synthesis had, perhaps, better
fortune. If Innocent III and St. Louis of France are
the most distinguished figures of political history
(which is also at this time the history of church-
organisation), their merit, as they would have eagerly
agreed, was more than counterbalanced by the
majestic figure of St. Thomas Aquinas. In the ninth
century John the Scot had attempted a theological
synthesis which, since it roamed far and wide over the
universe and contained so much speculation, is scarcely

[1] Lagarde, op. cit., pp. 494 ff.
[2] Lindsay, *History of the Reformation* I, pp. 216 ff.

to be recognised as such. St. Thomas Aquinas substituted reason for the experience and speculation of
John the Scot, and in his *Summa Theologica* and *Summa
Contra Gentiles* gave the world the greatest monument
of pure reason it has ever seen.

St. Thomas has a finality denied to any other
theologian of history, in that his use of pure reason is
directed to the single end of establishing the point at
which reason must abdicate. His way was prepared by the fresh wisdom of Anselm (1033–1109)
and in another way by the rebellious genius of Abélard
(1079–1142) ; still more immediately it was prepared by the perversions of the Arab Aristotelians,
Avicenna (980–1036) and Averrhoes (1126–98),
whose demonstrations by pure reason that much traditional Christian doctrine was untenable had done
great damage in the newly-formed intellectual circles
of their time. St. Thomas built a fortress of pure
reason on the very frontier of the enemy country by
employing the same Aristotelian methods which they
had employed, by out-thinking them in ruthless reason,
and by proving them, in inescapable terms, mean and
unprofitable. His synthesis of theology was, therefore, not only synthesis but also polemic. It gathers
up in itself the mountainous conflict as well as the
majestic monism of the Middle Ages. It has now
become the supreme source of Catholic learning ;
but it was not so regarded in the years immediately
following its composition. It came too late to be the
rational salvation of the Church's confusion.

Perhaps it is Dante (1265–1321), in his *De
Monarchia*, which he wrote in the early years of the
fourteenth century, who most aptly summarises the

situation. He tells us in that work that no synthesis between the Church and the state is possible ; that the Caesar-pope and the Papal prince are alike of no account. Augustine's monism must give way to a practical dualism ; temporal and spiritual must separate, although by this separation they will find that they are indispensable to each other. But if St. Thomas was too late, Dante, a generation after him, had little chance. Popes increased in worldly ambition, and not a few in worldly vice. The Papal Exile to Avignon (1309–78) and the Papal Schism (1378–1417, when two popes reigned simultaneously at Avignon and Rome) shattered the unity of the Church. Politics degenerated into plunder and the Black Death (1349) decimated the armies of church and state and culture. The unity of Europe was now the might of the strongest, and the vision of " order " receded into the far distance. The door was left wide open for that Byzantine humanism which, invading the West in the years following 1453, burst the restraining bonds of the decaying ecclesiastical system.

But even if synthesis was broken at the moment which might have been its final achievement, there is in the thirteenth century the nearest approximation that any age provides to a Christian culture. Everything of importance that was done in realms other than the narrowly political was done by the Church's sanction. Even that which was done in defiance of the church was done in open defiance. The distinction between " sacred " and " secular " was at this time no more than a distinction between the eternal and the temporal (*saeculare*). And that which was done without specific reference to the church or its teaching, such as (in our context) the music of the Troubadours and Trouvères, the court musicians of medieval Europe, was so clearly derived logically from the Sacred and not independent of it that we can without too much inaccuracy speak of the civilisation of this time as a Christian civilisation, and can with greater confidence than in any other age speak of " The Church " as acting and speaking through its representatives as a unity. We shall be considering in a moment a remarkable example of the phenomenon of " The Church " speaking about music.

(*b*) MUSICAL DEVELOPMENTS, 1100–1325

The dramatic appearance of " Sumer is icumen in ", the earliest and most celebrated of medieval *rotae*,[1] distinguishes the thirteenth century as being no less important in the history of music than it is in the history of Europe. " Two centuries ahead of its time " it ushers in the age of polyphony, and the period through which we are about to pass is the period during which music passes from the virgin perfection of " Sumer is icumen in " to the angelic maturity of the Golden Age of polyphony, through two centuries of uncomfortable adolescence.

We must not trace that history in any detail here. But since the " adolescence " of music included certain phases which caused the Church acute concern, we must attend to a few important points concerning the evolution of polyphony.

---

[1] *Rota* : a canon in which the voices enter successively with the same melody (in modern language a " round "), to be distinguished from *Rondellus* : a canon in which the voices enter simultaneously beginning at different points in the common melody. (See Reese, op. cit., p. 396.)

Polyphony (and by polyphony at its best we mean the music of the sixteenth century composers Palestrina, Byrd, Tallis and Lassus) has its origin in the confluence of two distinct streams of musical history, The first of these streams, whose course we are able to trace with tolerable certainty, leads back to the *organum* which was mentioned at the end of the last chapter. (The history is the more traceable since it was only the religious who were at that time capable of setting down musical theory and history on paper).

Consider a simple plainsong melody sung by two voices a fifth apart. Let the upper voice be the *vox principalis* or leader, and the lower the *vox organalis* of " second " voice. Suppose (to simplify the illustration by positing an extremely unlikely case) that the melody is in the key of C ; and then observe what happens when the " leader " reaches the note F. The " second " is immediately placed in a dilemma. If it follows the leader faithfully it must sing B flat, which is not a note in the scale on which the leader is singing ; if it keeps to the notes of that scale, however, it must sing B natural, which makes with the leader's F the harshest discord in the diatonic scale—the diminished fifth, or " tritone ". Since music does not willingly tolerate ugliness, the tritone is avoided at all costs in music of this period. Two courses are then open to the " second " voice. The simpler is to introduce the new note—B flat and continue in perfect fifths with the upper voice ; the result of this will be that to the monotony of perfect fifths will be added the piquancy of a " false relation " between the lower voice's B flat and the leader's B natural which will no doubt occur in the course of the piece. The more adventurous course is for the " second " voice to follow a line which is not directly congruent with that of the upper voice. The result of this is the beginning of independence between parts, that is, polyphony.

Now the employment of intervals other than fourths and fifths for the purpose of avoiding the tritone was called " free " *organum* and the device appeared early in the history of *organum*.[1] At first the main movement of the melodies was still in fifths and fourths, but intermediate intervals and " passing-notes ", carrying no musical emphasis but serving to help turn the awkward corners in the melody, appear in more and more variety until, as was inevitable, we find the principle that more than one note of *organalis* may be sung against one of *principalis* is accepted as a proper basis of development.

In a very early example of this, quoted by Reese[2] as from the school of Martial (early twelfth century), we see a free melody supported by a *cantus* of seven long notes ; each long note supports the interval of a fifth, but between the long notes the melody wanders through many other intervals. Moreover, the piece continues with the simultaneous singing of two different texts, and is in fact one of the earliest examples of this practice on which the church frowned heavily for a long time.

The other stream from which polyphony derived its origin is that of secular music, and here we are in the atmosphere of speculation and even guesswork which is proper to the examination of a tradition which was

[1] See page 86.
[2] Op. cit., p. 266.

G

almost entirely oral and not at all theoretical or written. "Sumer is icumen in" appears to us as a dramatic and sudden incursion of polyphony into secular music. Its immediate predecessors are unknown, and the explanation for its appearance in about the year 1240 has never been attempted. All that can be gathered from the shadowy evidence at our command is that in secular music a mysterious revolution took place about this time which placed secular music, for a time, at least a century ahead of religious music in its development. Whether this was due to the repressiveness of Christian public opinion we are unable to say, but we find in secular music the use of parallel thirds and sixths long before they come to be tolerated in sacred music. a comparison between parallel fifths and parallel thirds as a medium of musical expression shows what a spectacular innovation this was.

It appears that the centre of this activity in secular music was Great Britain. *Sumer is icumen in* is the proud possession of southern England and the Welsh theologian and writer on music, Geraldus Cambrensis (1146–1220) tells us of the practice of singing in thirds and sixths which, he says, is the common practice of Welsh singers in his time, but of which we have no record in any earlier authority.

These two streams—the sacred through free *organum* and the secular through the *rotae*—converge to produce polyphony, and when the church itself was emerging from the stagnation of the Dark Ages it found itself having to deal with a music that had been transformed by a process comparable with the discovery of a new dimension.

(c) THE ATTITUDE OF THE CHURCH

Contemporary criticism seems to show that the church was caught by the new music, if not unawares, at any rate in a condition of preoccupation with other issues. We have very little evidence of the reception which *organum* had in the church at large ; musicians who write as such and not as keepers of church-discipline write of it with enthusiasm, and the writings of the theorists show how much their subject-matter was enriched by this new development. A phrase in the *Musica Encheiriadis* quoted by Reese[1] suggests either that the attitude of the church authorities was not immediately friendly or that the writer was defending himself in advance against any prejudice which the authorities might feel.

But this gives us little either way. Much more interesting is the *De Musica* of Johannes Cotto[2] (usually thought to be an Englishman, John Cotton), in which we have a painstaking attempt to give a Christian lead in musical criticism. Nothing seems to be known of Cotton beyond the inference from his presence in the Patrologies that he held some position in the Church. His date can only be given by the vague deduction from internal evidence that he was writing in the twelfth century.

His most important concern (or at all events that which concerns us most in this enquiry) was with the "renewal" or reform of church-music. This leads him inevitably into the already well-worn topic of what is good and what is bad for church use. He bases his criticism in the first instance firmly on Platonic

[1] Op. cit., p. 255.
[2] Migne, *P.L.* C:, 1417 ff.

categories, and is quite happy to accept the notion
that certain modes, because of their qualities, are less
suitable than others for the expression of sacred
sentiments. But in the course of his argument it
becomes clear that the Platonic categories do not
account for all that he has to say. He writes at length
on technical blemishes which he feels are to be avoided
in church music, such as the setting of unimportant
syllables to long melodic flourishes and the musical
equivalent of the prosodic vice called *homoioteleuton*
(that is the cacophonous collocation of words or musical
phrases with similar endings : he mentions as examples
in words *Deus meus* and *Refugium meum*, and applies
the same criticism to musical phrases). He is moreover much concerned that the music shall be suitable
to the words it carries, and he goes into this question
with some thoroughness. It is impossible to read his
argument without feeling that he is recognising in the
music a source of individual character which is not
confined to the quality of the musical mode in which
it is written. We cannot be certain, but it may be that
in Cotton we have the first notions of the fact that
music can in its own right " say " something ; that
it can be a language not only of generalised emotion
but of argument, and that when the suitability of a
piece of music to certain words is being discussed there
are other matters to be reckoned with than the simple
approbation or condemnation of the mode of the music.
Certainly, now that *organum* and its derivatives have
come to stay, his subject-matter is greatly enlarged.
The wisdom and moderation of his criticisms may be
judged from the quotations we give from his work[1];

[1] Quotations 29 and 30, page 239.

he seems to advocate the kind of improvement which the uninitiated would scarcely notice but which would make the difference between the tedious and slovenly and the vital and true.

Less interesting but not negligible is the *De Musica* of Aribo Scholasticus (d. 1078), a typical example of the painstaking and systematic research into the mathematical properties of music which the theorists of the time undertook. Plato and Pythagoras are entirely responsible for its principles of criticism.

The real storm broke, however, over part-singing, and in the controversy which culminated in the Papal Edict of 1325 we may distinguish at least the following three issues : (1) part-singing in general, (2) profane music, and (3) the Hocket.

(1) Here is a generalised comment on the new elaboration of music from John of Salisbury (1115–80).

" Music defiles the services of religion ; for the admiring simple souls of the congregation are of necessity depraved—in the very presence of the Lord, in the sacred recesses of the Sanctuary itself —by the riot of the wantoning voice, by its eager ostentation, and by its womanish affectations in the mincing of notes and sentences."[1]

It should not escape the reader's notice that this, and other attacks on music (of which we give a further example in the Appendix[2]) comes from an author who was unquestionably an ancestor of English Protestantism. John of Salisbury is chiefly distinguished, in the very work from which these quotations come, by his

[1] Policraticus I. 6.
[2] Quotation 31, page 240.

concern at the exalted claims which the Papacy had
assumed ever since the accession of Hildebrand. His
defence of the rights of the common man are the
political counterpart of his condemnation of musical
elaboration which misleads and confuses the " simple
souls of the congregation ". We shall hear more of
this attitude when we attend to the English Puritans.

(2) But worse than this was to come. The
perverse developments of free *organum* are thus described in the most lively of modern text-books on
music :

"But the question may be asked ' What was
the church doing all this time ? ' Well, apparently
the church was doing very badly. When the world
turned topsy-turvy and people first realized that
music was not carpentering in 3-inch lengths, a
sort of licentious orgy set in. It is difficult to
explain with reverence just what happened. But
if the reader wishes a modern analogy with the
state of church music at that time, he may imagine
one of our church composers taking for his bass an
Anglican chant and spreading it out so that each
note occupied three or four bars ; then for his
treble using *Take a pair of sparkling eyes* (allegro
molto) ; and for his alto part fitting in as much as
he could of *Tipperary* or *Onward Christian Soldiers*,
or both. What the church service sounded like
under these conditions can be better imagined than
described. It *has* been described by contemporary
sufferers, and if half of what they say is true it must
have been like rag-time gone mad."[1]

[1] C. V. Stanford and Cecil Forsyth : *A History of Music* (1940), pp.
138 ff. Our epithet applies especially to that part of the book which is
the work of Forsyth.

This delightful summary of the conditions prevailing when secular music and musical devices intruded on the territory of sacred music spares us the need for further comment. It is upon this that the " puritans " of the time commented so unfavourably, and it is with such excesses that they associated part-singing.

(3) But the focus of the whole controversy was undoubtedly the " hocket ", a musical device whose name Forsyth says is cognate with the more familiar word " hiccough ", and which we must here explain.

Walter Odington, the greatest of the medieval theorists (another Englishman), who flourished about 1300, has this definition of the hocket :

" A truncation is made over the tenor . . . in such a way that one voice is always silent while another sings."[1]

In other words, instead of giving the counter-melody to a single voice, the composer divides it note by note between two or more voices. Almost certainly the origin of this device was secular and its unusual effect was used without offensiveness in the French *chaces*, or hunting songs, of the thirteenth century. Philippe de Vitry (1291–1361), composer, poet and diplomat, of whom we shall say more in the next chapter, appears to have exploited its dramatic powers and the most distinguished use of it in a religious context is, no doubt, the *Hoquetus David* of Gulielmus Machaut (1300–77). But the device carried more possibilities of abuse than could safely be left in the hands of these musicians. In any music written in the hocket-style, the melodic line of any single voice is

[1] A full account of this device will be found in Reese, op. cit. pp. 320 ff.

punctuated by rests ; indeed, the hocket is perhaps
the first instance of the deliberate use of the musical
rest as a dramatic agent.   But musical " aposiopesis "
of this kind clearly gives the chance for effects which
can only be described as fantastic at best or vulgar at
worst.[1]   Forsyth makes the following characteristic
comment : " From the many indignant protests of
the church-authorities that have come down to us
there is little doubt that the ' hocketting ' was often
not far short of scandalous. . . . The vile practices
against which churchmen exclaimed were not merely
musical ornaments and elaborations, but things of a
much more disreputable nature.   It is perhaps as well
not to enquire too closely what they were."

Here is a comment of Aelred of Rievaulx (d. 1166)
which indicates the concern which " hocketting "
was already giving to the churchmen of the twelfth
century :

> " Sometimes thou mayest see a man with open
> mouth, not to sing, but as it were to breathe out his
> last gasp, by shutting in his breath and by a certain
> ridiculous interception of his voice to threaten
> silence, and now again to imitate the agonies of a
> dying man, or the ecstasies of such as suffer."[2]

A more general comment on the new music comes from

---

[1] In the late string-quartets of Beethoven this very principle is
applied with remarkable results.   In the A major movement of the
Quartet in C sharp minor (op. 131) a single melody is divided between
two instruments, and the classic expression of musical " aposiopesis "
or the expressive use of rests is in the Cavatina of the B flat Quartet
(op. 130).   At certain dramatic points in the *Mass in D* rests appear
in the middle of phrases given to single words (for example, in the
Amens at the end of the Credo).

[2] See Reese, op. cit., p. 321.

a contemporary of Odington, Jean de Muris (fl 1300-25)

> " It really seems that certain persons only sing
> motets and songs in order to disfigure them with
> their hockettings.   They have allowed many other
> songs to fall into disuse ; they do not use, as our
> fathers did, songs in measured or partly-measured
> *organum*, the pure *organum* or the *organum* with the
> double, of which probably few of the present
> generation know anything."[1]

Here we have a fourteenth-century writer looking back
on *organum* with doubles (that is, the upper voice
which so soon became a free and even florid part)
as a staid and respectable device which the moderns
would do well to copy.

We may further quote John Wyclif (d. 1384),
whose political views were a considerable advance on
those of John of Salisbury, and who writes in a typically
" puritan " fashion on part-singing and the hocket :

> " In the old days, men sang songs of mourning
> when they were in prison, in order to teach the
> Gospel, to put away idleness, and to be occupied
> in a useful way for the time.   But those songs and
> ours do not agree, for ours invite jollity and pride,
> and theirs lead to mourning and to dwelling longer
> on the words of God's Law.   A short time later
> vain tricks began to be employed—discant, contre
> notes, organum, and hoquetus (small brekynge,
> which stimulate vain men more to dancing than to
> mourning. . . . When there are forty or fifty
> in a choir, three or four proud and lecherous rascals

---

[1] *Speculum Musicae* VII 44.

perform the most devout service with flourishes so that no one can hear the words, and all the others are dumb and watch them like fools."[1]

We may observe in this testy comment a certain impatience with the writer's subject-matter ; his indiscriminate condemnation of *hoquetus* along with *organum* indicates that he thought music too far gone in sin to deserve any more careful criticism.

But the most remarkable event, and the climax of the battle of the new music, is the edict of Pope John XXII which he promulgated in 1325[2] impressly forbidding extravagances in church music. The general sense of the edict (of which a translation is given at Quotation 32, page 249) is that whereas in the days of the Fathers church music was modest and restrained, and therefore conducive to a worshipful attitude in hearer and performer, the new music, employing modern techniques, has grown rank and extravagant. Without demanding that music be unduly fettered or restricted in its methods of expression, the Pope ordered that it be kept within proper bounds, that plainsong be restored to its place of honour, and laid down penalties for those who neglected to see this was done.

Now the edict in itself is a sane and moderate document, and the demands that it makes are in no way unreasonable. But the reader will not have failed to observe that Wyclif's splenetic outburst quoted above can scarcely have been made before the Edict, and was most probably made fifty years after it. The

---

[1] J. Wyclif, *Sermon on the Feigned Contemplative Life*.

[2] Until recently the date was held to be 1322 ; we follow Reese in accepting the later date.

fact is that the Edict had very little effect on church music in general. Here and there we find evidence that the Pope's wishes were taken seriously, (a document in Notre Dame, Paris, dating from 1408 shows an obedient temper in the chapter of that church)[1]. But the history of music shows that the disappearance of these extravagances, the hocket and all its attendant improprieties, from church music must have been due far more to the natural evolution of music and taste than to the arbitrary edict of the Pope.

Church history bears this out. Pope John XXII acceded (1316) when the Papacy had begun to decline in prestige and popularity after the " golden age " of Innocent III. To this decline more forces contributed than we can even mention here. The development of the Inquisition in 1252 into a tribunal which could torture as well as punish, the seriously depleted Papal treasury, the Papal exile to Avignon, not to mention the personal character and repressive policy of John XXII himself, were among these forces. His authority was of the cast-iron kind which was necessary in order to recover the economic prestige of the Papal throne, but which was not calculated to strengthen its spiritual hold on its empire. And in Europe at large, and especially in England, feeling was rising against the oppressiveness of papal authority. (A small but significant pointer is the fact that torture under the Inquisition was applied only once on English soil, at the trial of the Templars, 1309–11). Any text-book of church history will supply the evidence

[1] F. L. Charlier, *L'Ancien Chapitre de Notre Dame de Paris* (Paris, 1897), p. 67, quoting Jean Charlier, Advice to Choirmasters, 1408.

for a judgment that the year 1325 was not a propitious one for the promulgation of any edict which intended to carry plenary papal authority to the ends of the empire. Thus it was that in Europe and especially in England music, which had now been so radically transformed, continued in its own way.

It may well be argued, indeed, that with the best will and the highest authority in the world no pope could by edict have checked the development of music at this critical stage. There could be no going back on the invention of polyphony, which was an event in the "natural history" of music. Gregory the Great had been able to discipline a music which tended to extravagance in one technical dimension only—that of melody. And Gregory knew his subject intimately, a compliment which we cannot as safely pay to John. Music has, by the fourteenth century, burst the bonds of repressive criticism and calls for a treatment as different from that as is the discipline applicable to an adult and responsible person from that applicable to a young child. Upon this the Counter-Reformation has a lesson to which we must now attend.

CHAPTER V

THE RENAISSANCE AND THE REFORMATION

The meaning of *Renaissance*—The progress of Music—The Reformers and Music—The Counter-Reformation.

(a) THE MEANING OF "RENAISSANCE"

It is now generally regarded as misleading to attempt to "date" the Renaissance. The reason for this is that the Renaissance is an event which touches history in more than one plane. In one sense the date of the fall of Byzantium, 1453, when the culture of the East was released into the West by the great procession of refugees from the Turks, serves well enough as an "official" date. And yet in another sense, each art and mode of thought appears to have a "renaissance" of its own at some date between 1300 and 1600, but all different. Thirdly, "Renaissance", meaning "rebirth," has a connection with that supernatural history which is theological or metaphysical history. It is necessary for us to sort out, as far as we may, the complexity of this manifold idea before we attempt to speak of its particular manifestations in theology and music.

As an event in recorded history, then, the Renaissance is that phenomenon in art, letters, politics, and religion which had its immediate cause in the spilling-over of Byzantine culture into Europe after 1453. The importance of this single event must not be minimised. There is no doubt that, despite the stirrings of humanism in Europe well before that time and the evidence which we shall bring in a moment to show that to date the Renaissance in 1453 is not to tell the whole story, none the less had it not been for this Byzantine irruption, there would probably never have been an event significant enough to receive such a label at all.

But now consider the Renaissance as an event in the *natural* history of certain modes of thought. Its outward manifestations are a new exuberance and enthusiasm, and a break with a long tradition. These manifestations appear in all branches of human public activity. In the world of painting, there burst upon the world in the second half of the fifteenth century a new and noble efflorescence which we associated with such names as Botticelli (1447–1510), Leonardo da Vinci (1452–1519), and Michelangelo (1475–1564). In architecture there comes a clean break with Gothic style in favour of classical ideals in Bramante (1444–1514). And yet it is believed by many that the way for the Renaissance in painting was prepared by Giotto two centuries before (1266–1337). It is similarly believed, though with less confidence, that the new scientific awakening led by Francis Bacon (1561–1626) and Galileo (1564–1642) was prepared by Roger Bacon, again in the thirteenth century (1214–94). In letters there is little doubt that Petrarch (1304–74) leads the way into the same movement. Music is in a different case altogether and we will deal with it later.

If we lay alongside these manifestations in art the humanist theology associated in the first instance with

Erasmus (1466–1536) and the movements in politics in which in their various ways and contexts such pioneers as John of Salisbury, Marsiglio of Padua (c. 1270–1343), William of Ockham, and John Wyclif (d. 1384) (not to mention Wat Tyler) expressed their opposition to the plenary claims of the ecclesiastical empire, we see in the whole movement a single sentiment being reiterated and driven home from all sides. This is the claim that man shall be, not a pawn on the chessboard of popes or princes, but an object of reverence in his own right. This is humanism, and humanism its the keynote of the Renaissance. The new appreciation of the pagan classics, taking over from the Christian classicists of pre-Gregorian times, the new pride in human achievement, and the new claims for human freedom in politics and in scientific speculation all arose from this single source.

But when we have said this we have not reached the heart of the matter. What was behind this " humanism " ? Why is the phenomenon called a Renaissance ? " Renaissance " means rebirth. What had died ?

The answer to this question may perhaps be approached by way of an illustration. If any single figure can be easily accepted as symbolic of the Renaissance at its noblest, it is that of Leonardo da Vinci, who remains renowned in history as a man who surpassed all others in the startling diversity of his talents. Equally symbolic of the Middle Ages at their best is St. Thomas Aquinas, whose claim to be so regarded we have already hinted at. St. Thomas is venerated as one who gathered all things under the supreme science of theology. If the two figures be compared we see at once the real difference between the thirteenth century and the fifteenth. St. Thomas is intensive, Leonardo extensive. Leonardo " did everything ", explored everything ; St. Thomas called everything to order. St. Thomas was neither painter nor sculptor nor anatomist nor engineer ; but beauty and truth, health and reason have their place in the *Summa*. The monism of the Middle Ages can be summed up in the single word " Obedience ", and the leaping imagaination and vigour of the Renaissance in the word " Achievement ".

" Renaissance ", we may now repeat, means re-birth. Now " rebirth " happens to be a technical term of Christian spiritual theology. It means, as it is expounded in *St. John* iii, what happens to a man when, by an act of renunciation called " faith " he allows himself to be admitted to a life built on dimensions wholly other than those on which his natural life is built ; a life " in Christ" so different from the life which is not "in Christ" that it is natural to think of the difference in terms of " life " and " death ". Or, to put it in another way (equally Scriptural in authority), " rebirth " is the result of allowing the Word of God in Christ to kill something in oneself ; what He has killed is one's " right to be right ", one's natural tendency to trust one's own powers to save oneself and to achieve reality for oneself (I am deliberately using language as little emotive and as little technically spiritual as possible, for obvious reasons). The act by which a man allows the Word to do this killing (which has to be done constantly as upon a malignant growth) is known as Repentance.

Now this " rebirth " of which we are speaking was not of that kind. But it was the conviction of a whole continent of inquiring Christian minds, even though it was never expressed in such terms by any individual among them, that something had died and must be allowed to live again. They believed that man had died and that he had been killed by the Church. They believed (we continue to abstract corporate propositions from a history which justifies them in every page) that man, considered as a human being made in the image of God, must come alive again, and that his new life would be in some way better than the old one. Therefore in letters they went back behind Gregory I to the classics, Christian and pagan. In art, though they painted pictures of religious subjects almost exclusively, they proceeded on the assumption that art had for some reason been retarded and must now make up its lost ground. In politics they protested more and more loudly against the medieval synthesis, and in theology even the Catholics, and much more the Reformers, tossed St. Thomas aside and began to think their problems through afresh from Scripture and the early Fathers. The medieval synthesis had hardened (nowhere more than in its most visible aspect—the organisation of the church) into something like a prison ; the glory of obedience and renunciation, shown in the lives of the medieval saints as much as in the rational renunciation of St. Thomas, collapsed into oppression, and Martin Luther broke out of his monastery.

In all this there was not yet a hint of paganism ; the reaction was of Christians against a Christian error.

It was not even heresy. But neither was there in it any repentance.

The supernatural importance of the Reformation was that it was the voice of many prophets crying " Repent ". If Obedience had been the key-word of the Middle Ages and Achievement that of the Renaissance, " Forgiveness " was the key-word of the Reformation. Martin Luther and John Calvin, Philip Melanchthon and Huldreich Zwingli had a greater task even than John Hus and Savonarola. They had to proclaim not only the answer to the iniquity of Rome but also the answer to a Rebirth that knew no repentance. They proclaimed the rights of man's conscience and the downfall of medieval pomp as clearly as their predecessors, but they had also to warn those who, all unconscious of what was happening, were in danger of admitting seven devils where one had been before. The Reformation added repentance to the Renaissance and saved Europe from a new Dark Age. For it is not too much to say that had the Renaissance continued in its leaping achievements until the idea that the Church had stifled humanity had hardened into the cognate but monstrous idea (with which the present generation is, of course, familiar) that the Word of God had killed man, then the twentieth century would have been antedated by four hundred years ; for achievement without repentance, rebirth of the mind without voluntary spiritual death, is the fabric of confusion.

The achievement of the Reformation was to call a halt to the rising tide of humanism ; its secondary achievement was to make necessary the Counter-Reformation. If what has been said in the foregoing

pages is accepted as a true reading of those mighty
events, certain deductions about the evidences for
the church's views on music will follow without difficulty. We shall expect to find, and we shall indeed
find, nothing of any interest in the utterances of the
Church during the period of the Renaissance. The
church was in confusion, and man's achievement was
in full spate. From the Reformers we shall expect
many *obiter dicta* and a good deal of local precept ;
but since they were fighting for the life of the Faith,
they devoted their best energies, as was proper, to
questions which they thought more central than
music, and we shall find no coherent or connected policy
in them. We shall in fact find in them the pattern
of the change which after this chapter will have to
take place in the material of our study. But in the
Counter-Reformation we shall find something which
is probably more startling than anything since
Augustine's *De Musica*.

(b) THE PROGRESS OF MUSIC

But a few words are necessary on the development
of music during the Renaissance. The devices and
inventions which caused so much anxiety to John
XXII, and upon the development of which his edict
had so little effect, continued to flourish, and the music
of the fourteenth century, when there is added to the
hocket, the polyphonic technique, and the new
harmony the systematic use of notes of different
lengths, is compendiously known as *Ars Nova*. The
term itself is derived from a treatise by Philippe de
Vitry (d. 1361), but the earliest example of the division
of a breve into semibreves is to be found in a work of

Pierre la Croix which is dated 1298. Further divisions and sub-divisions of the breve followed quickly, and in the fourteenth century both France and Italy furnish examples of a music which has the full equipment in melody, notation, rhythm, and harmony, from which modern music is fashioned.

Now *Ars Nova* is not the Renaissance in music. The reader was warned that music does not follow the general pattern of things in this matter. *Ars Nova* is the logical development of music which can be traced back to the *organum*. Music is now *for the first time* an independent and responsible vehicle of expression. There is no *Renaissance* or rebirth about this. If we can speak of a Renaissance in music at all, it must be dated in about 1600 when Caccini and Peri produced in Italy the first operas. This is indeed a clean break with the tradition whose highest development is in Palestrina, and it is in a special way a new " humanism " in music.[1] But if it be regarded as a " Renaissance " in the sense of being the incursion of humanism, it is by no means a reaction against a played-out system. Nothing had been killed here. Palestrina, though the greatest, is not the last of his school, nor had any of these musicians even an obscure and unexpressed notion in their minds that the medieval synthesis had done music any damage. The historical fact is that music, developing so rapidly just as the medieval synthesis began to break down, snapped its fingers at the medieval synthesis altogether and therefore *a priori* released itself from any need of a " renaissance ".

But when all that is said, *Ars Nova* profited greatly

[1] See below, p. 146 f.

from the withdrawal of powerful restraint by the
church. In music both sacred and secular it
flourished. We have already mentioned an eminent
figure in France of this school, Guillaume de Machaut ;
he is the composer of the earliest known polyphonic
setting of the Mass. Another memorable name is that
of the Englishman Dunstable (c. 1370–1453), whose
school included Aleyn (d. 1396), Sturgeon, Burell,
Damett, and many others who have left some, if
fragmentary, evidence of their work.

It was not long before the new device of polyphony took to itself strange forms. The music of
the Flemish school, exemplified in the works of
Ockeghem (1425–95), Obrecht (1430–1505) and
Weerbecke (1440–?) abound in strange combinations of musical ingenuity such as mirror canons
(incorporating a melody which reads the same when
reversed) and " canon cancrizans " (in which the
second voice announces the reverse of the subject
announced by the first). These ingenious mechanisms
of musical mathematics appeal more to the admirer
of well-turned conundrums than to the *bona fide*
listener. But we hear nothing from the church on
the matter yet. And indeed it seems that the poly-
phonic technique was only outgrowing its strength
for a period. Its golden age hastens on, and in the
sixteenth century the names of Tallis (d. 1585),
Lassus (d. 1594) and Palestrina (1525–94) are
sufficient guarantee that polyphony has at last found
itself and come to a graceful maturity. That ingenuity
which the Flemish school carried to startling, if harmless, excess has its apotheosis in Tallis's majestic
forty-part motet, *Spem in alium*. All of this is a

continuous development, producing here and there mistakes and monsters but never breaking with tradition. And while the monastic houses and cathedral churches of Europe were singing the motets of Josquin des Près and Tallis, the common people, already feeling something of a new freedom from feudalism, a new mobility and aspiration of mind, were singing secular songs, in many of which music of matchless grace was allied with texts of rich impropriety.

(c) THE REFORMERS AND MUSIC

The reader was warned that we have nothing to report from Catholic authorities on music before the Council of Trent. But in the Reformers we have many examples of musical criticism to attend to.

First, of course, is Martin Luther (1483–1546), whose gesture in nailing the "ninety-five theses" to the churchdoor at Wittenburg on October 31st, 1517, is regarded as the opening of the Reformation. Luther's position in the history of Christian doctrine is best expressed by saying that more perhaps than any other important Christian teacher he had the genius and the failings of an artist. His enemies have not found it difficult to represent him as a monster of iniquity and especially of sensuality ; vicious caricature from the Roman church is quite unable to represent him, as it represents Calvin, as dry, heartless, and stonily puritanical, because his manner of life and thought was in truth the reverse of puritanical. Luther's theology was not a theology of negation ; by definition it was the opposite of a theology of legalism. In it there is no asceticism or monasticism; in his thought, indeed, there is too little discipline for it ever to be called a philosophy. His attack on the Church of Rome centred first on the matter of Indulgences, which he attacked with all his rhetorical power as a blasphemous travesty of the technique of the Forgiveness of Sins. He preached Justification by Faith, the theology of the Forgiveness of the Individual. He was an evangelical preacher and his whole concern was with removing the obstacles to the salvation of the simple which he believed the Church of Rome had deliberately put in his way. Everything else was subservient to this message of Reconciliation. His politics and the other parts of his theology, inconsistent and often hastily-conceived as they were, were only there to make straight the way for Forgiveness. In this he was a prophet, not a philosopher. He was the reverse of systematic because he was so passionately devoted to the single idea. His liturgical reforms, therefore, expressed so far as he could make them do so his belief in the goodness of things human and the sanctity (or rather the destiny of sanctification) of the human soul.

He therefore gathered music into the service of the church. The richness and drama of the Roman Mass he long wished to retain ; it was only gradually that he found sweeping changes necessary. It was not he, indeed, who first insisted on the Mass being sung in the vernacular. But in as much as the purpose of the Mass was to make straight the way of the people's salvation, he taught the people to sing. A musician himself, he composed or caused to be composed a whole *corpus* of chorales which form the basis of all

Lutheran church song to the present day.[1] Polyphony and elaboration he loved in themselves, but they are not music for the people. His liturgical music therefore follows the pattern of the broad unison song, very often founded on a secular melody.

As a critic of church music, therefore, Luther is a good example of a new " positive " approach to music. He selects from the available resources that which is strictly suitable for his purpose without troubling to criticise that which he does not select. He wants his people to join in the singing, and so he devises a musical form that they can sing as their own part in the service. But he loves music too well to indulge in the kind of moralistic criticism of which we saw much in earlier times. The one matter on which he seems to have a strong adverse view is the use of the organ in church. Albert Schweitzer in his *J. S. Bach* says this :

" We may read through all Luther's writings without finding a single place where he speaks of the organ as the instrument accompanying congregational singing. Moreover he, the admirer of true church-music of any kind, gives no directions as to how the organ is to co-operate in the service. It really is incredible, however, that in the few places where he mentions the organ at all, he speaks of it almost scornfully : he does not look on it as necessary or even desirable in the evangelical

---

[1] Many well known hymn-tunes date from this period. It is not certain whether *Ein Feste Burg* and *Vom Himmel hoch* (E.H. 362 and 17) are Luther's own compositions ; but *Innsbruck* and *The Passion Chorale* (*ib.* 86, 102) are certainly derived from secular melodies.

service, but at most tolerates it where he finds it already."[1]

This, of course, is a quotation from a modern church musician and organist. Perhaps Luther's neglect of the organ is not difficult to understand if it be remembered, first, that organs in those days were exceedingly primitive and, to the discerning ear, not apt to beautify the service in the way to which our own generation is accustomed, nor to do more than support the pitch of the singers ; and secondly, that the practice of the day was in any case to sing church music *a cappella* and that we continue to hold that accompaniment on an instrument destroys the beauty of sixteenth century polyphony. Luther's neglect of the organ, in fact, is neglect and not positive criticism of the kind which the early Fathers levelled at the flute and which the later Puritans certainly aimed at the organ. We shall encounter more positive criticism of organ-accompaniments in a moment.

Luther's view of church music was supported by Philip Melanchthon (1497–1560) who writes :

" When church music ceases to sound, doctrine will disintegrate. Religious music applied to life is a sanctification of life."

In so writing Melancthon expresses his sympathy with the traditional view that music of the right kind can actively do good to the worshipper.

In Switzerland, on the other hand, we have a very different atmosphere. The German Reformation, under Luther, Melancthon, and Bucer, is always moderate ; the goodness of the Roman tradition is,

[1] English Edition, I 94.

one feels, always let go with regret. The widening
gulf between Luther and the Pope, together with the
political complications which add so much tragic
confusion to the scene of the Reformation, is responsible for reforms and reactions far more violent
than Luther ever envisaged in the early days at
Wittenburg. The rites of Strasbourg compiled by
Bucer show a strong independence of Rome, and yet
a broad sympathy with the real basis of medieval
Christian worship which is absent from the Swiss
atmosphere.

Huldreich Zwingli (1484–1531) of Zurich was,
in contrast to Luther, a fighter who lost his own life
in a religious war. His reforming zeal was not embarrassed by any of Luther's humanistic craving for
the beautiful or regret for what had to be left behind if
the Roman Mass was discarded. Zwingli is the only
one of the Reformers who made an effort to dispense
with music altogether. He abolished it in 1525
from the rite he prepared for Zurich, and substituted
the antiphonal recitation of psalms and canticles.
W. D. Maxwell[1] states his own doubt whether the
abolition of music ever proved successful and whether
the discipline continued long. "Before the end of
the sixteenth century", he adds, "Zurich had
abandoned the extreme view that led to the exclusion
of music from worship, and introduced congregational
singing ".

Zwingli's liturgical reforms in general were not
only radical but also such as proceeded from a purposeful but prosaic mind. His hatred of Rome was
intense, and his grasp of the more subtle issues involved

[1] *An Outline of Christian Worship*, p. 86.

was incomplete. The attitude he adopted to music springs from that narrowness of purpose which combined with limited imaginative apprehension, produced the memorialist emphasis in his doctrine of the Eucharist. But in all these things Zwingli was an exception even among Reformers, and neither his arid doctrines nor his liturgical disciplines were followed outside Zurich.

John Calvin (1509–64) is a far more subtle person than either Zwingli or Luther, and probably more grievously misunderstood by posterity. He sought to gather up Reformed teaching into a system and a discipline ; in his *Institutiones* he gave the system, in his church at Geneva the discipline. He combines the sternness of Zwingli with Luther's compassion more completely than his critics care to believe. The result in his theology and his liturgies is not aridity but power ; the power is that which comes not from catholicity, as in St. Thomas Aquinas, but from concentration. Therefore neither the theology nor the liturgies are in any sense the " last word " on their subject. They have in them inevitably something of the polemic, something of the exaggerated and the temporary, and much that later ages, if they wish to interpret the will that gave them birth, need to rephrase and re-think. But to say that as the ages pass Calvin's own doctrines need re-phrasing in order that they may become clear is not to say that the passing ages make it necessary to discard Calvin. It is only to say that the violence and heat of the sixteenth century in Geneva caused Calvin to express himself in a way that left him wide open to misunderstanding.

If Luther's theology was the theology of humanity

redeemed, and Zwingli's that of rationalism, Calvin's is the theology of the Sovereignty of God. Yet by a paradox which we may not here digress to explain, it was Calvin who had the better developed doctrine of democracy, and from whose teaching is derived the doctrine of Presbyterianism. His theology was not all doom. " Predestination " occupies three chapters in the final chapter of the *Institutes*, and is only there expressed in the stark fashion that has given so much offence to later generations. Consider this :

" Can we think that our Lord would have given to flowers such beauty as presents itself to our eyes, if it were not intended that we should feel pleasure as we look at them ? Let us therefore refuse to accept that inhumane philosophy which, refusing to concede to men any use of the good creatures of God, except on grounds of necessity, not only deprives us unreasonably of the unbidden fruit of divine beneficence, but also can only come into practice when, having robbed men of all sentiment, it has turned him, as it were, into a log of wood."[1]

Calvin was not the man to dismiss any category of creation as useless or evil. But his conviction of God's sovereignty and man's rebelliousness was complete. He believed in " total depravity " in the sense of saying that there was no activity in which man must not suspect himself of being infected by sin. And so everything, including music, was subjected to careful scrutiny. He disapproves of ornamental aids to worship of any kind as ends in themselves, imply-ing that to make and use them under the impression

[1] From the *Institutes*, cited in Scholes *The Puritans and Music*, o. 335.

that they are " a sacrifice of praise " is self-deception.[1]
But in another place he says that although the Church
has criticised the tabor and flute, it is not because of
their essential nature but because of man's abuse of
them.[2] What he does insist on is that there shall be

> " simple and pure singing of the divine praises,
> forasmuch as where there is no meaning there is no
> edification. Let them come from heart and mouth,
> and in the vulgar tongue. Instrumental music was
> only tolerated in the time of the Law (that is, the
> Old Testament) because of the people's infancy ".[3]

From this we can see that in Calvin, the most
systematic of the Reformers, the following points are
made with regard to music: (1) Music is for the
people, so it must be simple ; (2) Music is for God,
so it must be modest ; (3) These objects are best
attained by the music of the unaccompanied voice.
In other words, we are beginning to see a fairly well-
developed doctrine of " sacred music ". This is of
great importance.

During the sixteenth century Europe was, of course,
full of music of every kind, much of it, as we have
seen, secular. Nothing explicit is said anywhere on
the subject by Reformers or counter-reformers, but it
is quite clear that the fact that there is one music for
church and another for secular use is becoming
accepted. And the policy to which it gives rise in the
Reformed church is not so much the deliberate
avoidance of all secularism in church (Luther especially

[1] See Sermon 66, on I Sam. xix (David's harp).
[2] *Sermons on Job,* 79-80.
[3] Sermon 66.

loved to use the folk-melodies as the basis of his chorales) as the coining of a new form of church music. Before the Reformation, church music and secular music shared the whole vocabulary of music, harmony, polyphony, hoquetus, and the rest. Churchmen in criticism said in effect, " Music in church must not wear these extravagant garments ", but it did not say that it must get itself an entirely new set of garments. Luther and, even more, Calvin, did say just that. And the best argument against Calvin's ruthless intellectualism and heartless gloom is the Genevan Psalters which he caused to be musically edited by Louis Bourgeois and Claude Goudimel, in which the new musical form of the church's own invention is brought to its highest manifestation. This invention is the Psalm-tune, which became later the hymn-tune. Given this new form, Calvin saw to it that it was made as well as the best musicians available could make it. Here at last is positive criticism ; instead of directions what the church must not do with music we have in the reformers examples deliberately given of what the church shall do. They are saying not " That is wrong " but " This is right ".

If Calvin's insistence on God's sovereignty made him extremely fastidious about everything that the church offered to God and caused the music of the Genevan Psalters to be of the soundest that could be provided, his democratic convictions led to the severe discipline which made this music so essentially simple and memorable. The effects of this " democratic " aspect of Reformed teaching on churchmusic will come up for discussion in later chapters, but we will note here one by-product of it which appears in the Psalters. Simple music is memorable music, and music which can be remembered by a musically unskilled congregation depends entirely on *form*. It must consist of familiar phrases and, if at all possible, must contain either plain repetition or intelligible development of these phrases. If the reader turns to the melody of the first Psalm in the 1543 Genevan Psalter[1] he will see in it (1) a very solid, not to say modern, major tonality ; (2) a musical form well established by the repetition of the first line at the end and the development of the third line in the fourth ; and (3) a singularly simple and memorable "shape" in the tune caused by the placing of the one high note. This, which could easily defend the claim to be the greatest, and is certainly one of the first, of all hymn-tunes is, surely, a watershed between the wayward polyphony and tonality of the sixteenth century and the more restricted tonality and more intricate musical "form" and rhetoric of the eighteenth. This, then, is what Protestant criticism did for music in the sixteenth century.

(*d*) THE COUNTER-REFORMATION[2]

The rising tide of secularism in Europe in the sixteenth century, of which the musical was only one aspect, was a matter of concern to Catholics as well as to the new Protestants. The time came when the Catholic church felt that the Renaissance had gone far enough in the direction of division and decentralisation of autonomies, and, by no means blind to certain

---

[1] *Songs of Syon* (1910), 330.
[2] See Lang, *Music in Western Civilisation* (1942), pp. 226 ff.

excellent grounds which the Reformers had for their complaints, the Catholic Church gathered in Council at Trent in the year 1545. The Council continued through numerous sessions until 1563, and its findings were promulgated in 1570. It was a reforming Council, and in all the diversity of its various conclusions can be discerned the desire for co-ordination, for the drawing together of a church scattered and confused not only by the assaults of the Reformers but also by its own iniquity and the legacy of medieval sloth and luxury.

There is much in the Counter-Reformation that expresses reaction against the Renaissance. To take only a single example, the writings of St. Peter of Alcantara are full of exhortations to distrust and dismiss the things of this world which are more extravagant than any Puritan would have dared to commit to paper, and are directed precisely at the temper of mind, speculative, and undisciplined, which the Renaissance had engendered. The liturgical sessions of the Council of Trent were, in a similar way, concerned to purify church music from the associations of secularism. The twenty-second session of the Council, in 1562, contains a good deal of matter that bears on this enquiry.

The material before this session was in the form of a series of complaints about the condition of church-music. The singers behaved irreverently, they sounded their words slackly, the composers disregarded the text in their musical exuberance, the secular spirit in music was ubiquitous and unashamed, the use of instruments in church was altogether extravagant, and so on. These were all complaints with which John Calvin would have heartily agreed. The Council came to a preliminary decision in the following form :

> " Let them keep away from the churches those forms of music with which, either by the organ or by singing, anything lewd or impure is mixed, in order that the House of God may be truly seen to be the House of prayer."

But they went further than this. The moving spirit in the Council on this matter was one Otto, Cardinal Truchsess, Bishop of Augsburg. He commissioned his choirmaster, Jacobus de Kerle, to write for the council some simple settings of prayers, and during the sessions this music was performed. The music was, by sixteenth century standards, entirely undistinguished, employing polyphony and homophony in strict moderation. This, the avoidance of all those embellishments which had been the cause of offence, was exactly what was wanted. The *Preces Speciales* of de Kerle were heartily approved by the Council, and the Council were able to say, not merely that embellishments must in a general way be abolished, but that *this* was the kind of music they regarded as proper for use in Church. Once again, we have a new positive criticism as the answer to the failure of John XXII.

This, however, was only the first of several important steps taken by the Roman Church in the direction of the establishment of a " church-music " in the new sense. We now go beyond the twenty-second session of the Council of Trent, but not beyond the policy which it inaugurated, in telling the story of Orlando

I

de Lassus (sometimes Italianised as Orlando di Lasso) (1532–94). Lassus was a prolific and industrious composer ; at his death he left some two thousand works. For the first twenty years of his musical life he poured out a series of delicious madrigals, love-slongs, chansons, and secular music in all possible forms. In 1568 he received a commission to set to music the *Rime Spirituali* of Gabriel Fiamma, canon at the Lateran, which were poems written in the technique of secular poetry but upon sacred subjects ; in the preface the author claims to have " redirected Tuscan poetry, in as lofty a manner as possible, towards virtue and towards God ". So Lassus was brought in contact with the songs of the Church, and by 1576, his biographers say, he had renounced entirely the setting of secular words. From then until his death he turned out religious music with all the energy and all the graceful skill which he had been devoting to the secular. This " conversion " of Lassus cannot be said to be merely a move of policy by the Church. It is more than an event in the history of outward things. But the action of Fiamma in composing the *Rime Spirituali* and in commissioning this Flemish musician to set them to music shows the technique which the Roman Church used at this time for canalising the energy which was running to waste in secular pursuits.

A second musician to whom something of the same kind occurred was Victoria (c. 1540–1611), the Spanish musician who fell under the influence of the Society of Jesus. The Society, commonly known later as " the Jesuits ", was a typical result of the new spirit of the Counter-Reformation. Its founder,

Ignatius Loyola, had been a Basque soldier, and he organised the Society as a highly-disciplined company of Christian " shock-troops " who were committed to go wherever they might be sent to preach the Gospel and convert the heathen. Their greatest success was in Poland, which from that time has remained a solidly Catholic country. The temper of their discipline, mental and physical, can be seen in these words of Loyola :

> " Consummate prudence allied with moderate saintliness is better than greater saintliness and mere prudence."

Loyola himself disliked music ; he found it an unnecessary distraction, and forbade its use by his novices. Nevertheless the Society's college, the *Collegium Germanicum*, was near enough to the *Collegium Romanum* for some of the musical tradition of the latter institution to overflow into the Society ; and when the young Victoria entered the Collegium Germanicum in 1565 Palestrina was teaching at the *Romanum*. The story of Victoria's life is the story of a man who several times, under the influence of Jesuit intensity, was on the point of abandoning music for the priesthood. But he never did so, and was content to dedicate his musical talents, fertilised by Palestrina's genius, to the undivided service of the church.

But the story of Palestrina himself (1526–94) is perhaps the most remarkable of all. Palestrina was named after his native town (the ancient Praeneste of Pliny and Horace), and in that town he began his musical career. In the time of Pope Julius III

(1550–55) he became *magister puerorum* at the *Capella Julia* at St. Peter's. His first volume of Masses (1554) is dedicated to the Pope in gratitude for this appointment. A little later he was made a member of the Sistine Chapel choir ; but this appointment was found to be irregular since he was a married man, and the succeeding Pope, valuing the proprieties more than Palestrina's genius (as he was bound to do), cancelled the appointment. From 1555 to 1571 Palestrina's life was burdened with intrigue and ill-health, but in 1571 he was restored to the *capella Julia.* Pope Sixtus V (1585–90) tried to restore him to the Sistine chapel, but his clerical advisers would not countenance the irregularity. He was therefore compensated by the creation of a new official title—*maestro compositore.* From that time till his death in 1594 he was greatly honoured by the Church and regarded as its leading musician. The story of the Church's endeavours to keep his services and make the most of them, and of their fruit in the creation of this new office, is one more piece of evidence for the new spirit of positive criticism of music which we have seen all over Europe. There was no question here at all of telling Palestrina what to write. There is nothing inhibited or truncated about his music from beginning to end. Nor, as our own century is learning, is his music in any sense emasculated or " ethereal ". It is simply polyphony written under a voluntary discipline, and emerging with a power which none of his contemporaries ever came near to achieving. There is power and passion in Palestrina ; there is experience and expressiveness. (We need go no further than the opening homophony of *Stabat Mater*

for sheer disciplined pathos). It is the musical expression of the truth expressed in the phrase " Whose
service is perfect freedom ". As *maestro compositore*
Palestrina was set aside by the Church to do this.
The Church said in effect, " We will not waste time
directing what musicians shall not do. This we
regard as great music and as religious music. Let
Palestrina speak for himself and for us ".

(e) CONCLUSION

This brings us to the end of that part of our enquiry
which deals with the attitude of a united Church to
music. From this point onwards the enquiry will be
of a very different kind. We have, after the Reformation, no united church to draw on for material. Instead of being able to speak of " The Church and
music " even as intelligibly as we have been able to do
so far, we shall have to speak rather of " religious
history and music ". We shall only be able to trace
the important movements of religious experience
considered as movements in the history of God's
dealings with His people, and try to relate them with
movements in church music. Our conviction of the
existence of such a relation is the ground for proceeding
into the next chapter. But before we do so it will be
helpful to gather up a few conclusions that emerge
from the foregoing pages.

1. We found in the beginning that music, as a
natural activity of man and an object of speculation
and criticism, was one of the component parts of that
world of thought and experience into which the
Church was born. Moreover music had already
been found to be a means of expression. As such it

came under the criticism of the earliest authorities of the church, who sought to guide music into the expression of sentiments and truths appropriate to Christian public worship.

2. But all the criticism of the early Fathers, and the medieval criticism derived from it, was directed upon music considered as a vehicle for religious sentiment or a vehicle for secular sentiment ; music, that is, as the handmaid of poetry or at any rate of the spoken and thought Word. That music is also, and indeed primarily, a vehicle for the expression of truths which cannot be expressed by other means, and is to that degree autonomous, did not occur to the church-authorities until the development of *organum* and the commentaries on this development by the medieval theorists brought this fact to the church's notice. And even then such authorities as John XXII recognised not the cause but only the symptoms of the new freedom of music. Criticism up to the time of the Renaissance proceeds on the assumption that music can be fashioned and disciplined by reference to the liturgical needs of the church and without reference to its own nature. Criticism of music by modal categories died hard. Good and bad music was music suitable and not suitable to the human need for which it was being used. The notion of an internal or metaphysical goodness or badness in music was not entertained at all.

3. In the sixteenth century we see the church, both reformed and Catholic, abandoning the elementary forms of criticism and turning to a new line. The Reformers coined new sacred musical forms which had nothing in common with secular forms.

The Catholic church " baptised " the secular musicians into sacred uses : and the " baptism " had not a little of renunciation in it, so that both Catholics and Reformers, each party in its own way, were making a new distinction between sacred and secular. By pointing to the new music with approval rather than pointing to the old with condemnation they began a new tradition of " positive " criticism.

4. But to all of these tendencies Augustine remains an exception. His method of criticism is neither negative, nor, in the sense in which we have used the expression, positive, but metaphysical. He is concerned with music as an entirely autonomous object of study, and in his derivation of bad music from *superbia* he follows out the scholastic tradition of regarding music as responsible to no collateral force but as entirely dependent for its intelligibility and " goodness " on theological virtues. We have not yet come across any criticism that goes on from here.

PART TWO

FROM this point onwards the shape of our study must change. Even the meaning of our title, *The Church and Music*, must be understood in a new way. For we are now dealing with a church permanently in the condition of schism, which means that we can no longer speak of the Church as a unified and accepted authority in the sense in which it was both united and accepted until the end of the Middle Ages. During the five hundred years preceding the Reformation the Western Church had suffered much from heresy—the secession of individuals or groups on points of doctrine—but the body of Christian doctrine was not seriously harmed by heresy. Schism, or disciplinary secession, had been less in evidence ; even the so-called Eastern Schism (1054) was not purely a disciplinary issue. But if we say that by the explosion of the Reformation and the resulting schism of the church into many bodies all sharing the same basic beliefs but differing on points of church order Christian discipline was seriously harmed as doctrine had not been harmed by heresy, we must immediately qualify that statement by saying that in a sense neither the schism nor the secularism were in the relation of cause and effect to one another, but that they were parallel effects of the humanistic upheaval in the Renaissance. In the sixteenth century we are faced with a divided church and a sudden secularism, which condition prevails to the present day.

A divided church believing a single creed is a strange phenomenon for which we must make full allowance. Its result in our study will be seen clearly to be that while the church has no longer any central authority to play the part that the Pope played in the Middle Ages, yet the Church can be said to have in many things a " common mind ". The church loses its Roman focus through the collapse of universal discipline, but it by no means loses the inheritance of belief. Or, to put it in another way, in the sense of being an institution under a single temporal discipline the Church ceases to exist in the sixteenth century, but in the sense of being a Body to which a single doctrine is committed it continues to exist, and its office is carried out neither more nor very much less success-fully than it was carried out in the ages of unified discipline. Heresy continues through these later centuries, but it does not conquer. Schism persists, and is in our own time becoming increasingly seen to be a ground for penitence; but as between the Church of Rome, the Church of England, the English denominations affiliated to the Free Church Council, the Lutheran Church, and any other form of " ortho-dox dissent ", there are no credal differences in-corporated in these churches' charters or orders. The differences are disciplinary, and if it is clear that we may not regard the state of schism as a condition to be tolerated for ever, it is by no means so certain that the centuries of schism as we have known them have done any injury whatever to the body of Christian doctrine committed to the Church.

Introduction

Therefore we have to regard The Church from now on not so much as an event in natural or eventual history, as what it properly is, an event in supernatural history ; we have to take full advantage of the fact that there is in the church a supernatural character imparted by the supernatural character of that which is committed to it. We can turn this fact to good account by inferring from it that we may gather information for our study from the attitude and reaction of churchmen of every denomination to music, taking our material from many scattered sources which are technically out of communion with each other, and relying on such sources more heavily than on authoritative declarations from Papal or royal thrones ; and in proceeding thus we shall not be doing violence to our title. We can still speak of The Church as we regard the Church as essentially a Body which, in the words of Cyprian, " cannot be divided ".

And so the material to which we shall be attending will be of a different kind from that which was the material of our First Part. There we dealt with the writings of churchmen and the decisions of popes and councils. Here we shall be dealing rather with less tangible evidences such as the Puritan attitude to music, the use made of music in revivals, the odd phenomenon of bad music in the nineteenth century, and the evidences supplied by contemporary music and musical philosophy. The evidences we adduce will lack the universal quality of the documents of our earlier chapters. They will be partial, even provincial in character. We shall be fitting together a mosaic rather than drawing a single picture. What our nondocumentary evidences may be expected to furnish is a picture of the effect on musical thinking and practice produced by the stresses and tensions of church history. From this we may expect to gather some kind of converging testimony, not complete in any one place or age but accruing from the accumulation of evidence, which may lead us in the direction of Christian judgment about music.

CHAPTER VI

THE SEVENTEENTH CENTURY

The Heirs of the Reformation—The Established Church in
    England—The New Music on the Continent—The New
    Music in England.

(a) THE HEIRS OF THE REFORMATION

The latter half of the sixteenth century and the
whole of the seventeenth are memorable for the rise
and progress of the struggle between what we may
roughly call the Puritan and the Traditional world-
views. We use these terms in their widest sense,
to cover politics as well as theology. The legacy of
the Renaissance was individualism ; the achievements and potentialities of the single man were
vindicated in Leonardo, and what he stood for was
never allowed to be forgotten. Now Puritanism,
which is a large subdivision of Reformed churchmanship, is the outlook in religion and politics which most
emphatically stresses the primacy of freedom ; freedom, that is, from temporal authorities and restraints
in order that the Christian may have the chance to
obey the laws of the Kingdom. Puritanism, that is,
enjoins political and ecclesiastical freedom along with
strict obedience to the " Crown rights of the Redeemer ", Earthly laws must relax in order that the
laws of Grace may have full play. It is only a debased
Puritanism that degenerates into anarchy and political
agitation ; and the detractors of Puritanism had

better note that it is equally a debased Puritanism that gives all its time to the minute observance of obediences that claim to be of the Kingdom but are in fact of the world. It has been to the advantage of some who have polemical ends in view to represent Puritanism as the source of wider industrial anarchy and organised greed (see, for example, the writings of Hilaire Belloc), and of others less seriously inclined to represent it as the new Pharisaism, censorious and joyless (we think here of some of the less responsible utterances of the late G. K. Chesterton). It has indeed been possible for some of the " self-help " school of politics as for some of the Pharisaic temper in religion to find authority for their views in the superficially-studied works of Puritans here and there. But the fact remains that anarchy and joylessness are perversions of Puritanism. The Puritans at their best stood for freedom, and that freedom was the only kind worth standing for—freedom to obey the Word of God.

This led them, of course, to be extremely sensitive to all forms of generalised authority (though Cromwell's army was by no means intolerant of a specialised and purposeful obedience). More than this, the thoughtful Puritan was suspicious of anything whatever that might bemuse or defraud the individual believer. He insisted that the believer should be saved as a whole, free, and alert individual. And therefore the Puritan attitude to church music was just what we have seen to be the attitude of the church of the fourth century.

Now Puritan church music in England and Scotland—of which we have the best examples in the

Scottish Psalters—is rugged, simple, stern, and extremely limited in its technique. The Scottish Psalters,[1] which draw their life from the Genevan fountain-head by way of the Psalters of 1556 and the following years, consist almost entirely of common-metre hymn-tunes adapted from Genevan tunes or composed on the same model. The Puritans, following Calvin, suspected any music which was in the least complex ; they would not have polyphony,[2] and they abjured all complexity of metre in the psalm-versions. They would sing, of course, only Psalms. Hymns, being human compositions, they mistrusted since they wished to keep the authority of Scripture clear of human interference. (Indeed, during the seventeenth century scarcely any English hymns were written at all. The familiar hymns from that age are poems which their authors never designed for congregational singing.) The early Baptists, it is recorded, went further, and denied their congregations the use of books in congregational singing.[3] Instruments were, of course, forbidden altogether in church.

All this is common knowledge. But a study of the actual music which this severe discipline produced leads us to the conclusion that the discipline did no harm to the music. The number of psalm-tunes from the Scottish Psalters of 1615 and 1635 and Ravenscroft's English Psalter of 1621 that are in use to-day in Great Britain, some of them in common and universal use, is truly astonishing when the modest

[1] On this subject see Millar Patrick, *Four Centuries of Scottish Psalmody*, O.U.P., 1949.

[2] The first edition of the Psalms in Scotland to provide four-part harmony was Miller's of 1643.

[3] Percy Scholes, *Oxford Companion to Music*, s.v. *Baptist Church*.

number of compositions originally available in those books is remembered.[1] When a hymn-tune lasts for three hundred years, even with intermissions, its integrity may be guaranteed. The anonymous composers of these tunes were men of a spare but undeniable musical genius.

Now the music of Puritan Britain could not have achieved this integrity, this quality of soundness and truth, had the principle behind it been that music was to be suspected in itself. Had the composers of these tunes been aggressive amateurs who held that the music of the rest of the world was godless and to be avoided, nobody can say what the result would have been but they certainly would not have been tunes like *Dundee*, *York*, and *Martyrs*.[2] This is but subsidiary evidence to all that is provided by Dr. Percy Scholes in his astonishing book *The Puritans and Music*,[3] in which he proves as conclusively as any scholar ever succeeded in proving a case that there is nothing in seventeenth-century Puritanism in England or America to support the view that the Puritans objected to music *as such*, or to the performance of secular music in general. The case is made out so completely in that book that we may accept it here as it stands, and hold to our conclusion that Puritan criticism of music was not negative but positive : that is to say, the Puritan worship applied to church-music such disciplines as

[1] *Songs of Praise* (1931), a hymnal by no means biased in favour of Puritanism or of Scotland, contains sixteen tunes from the 1635 Scottish Psalter. Of twelve tunes in Andro Hart's 1615 edition, six remain in common use to-day.

[2] *Songs of Praise* (1931), 557, 628, 597.

[3] O.U.P., 1936.

it applied to everything else connected with the church, denying it the right to stand in the worshipper's way, but according it the right, subject to that, to *be music*. The high standard of composition in the early Psalters is sufficient proof that Puritan discipline was not repressive but creative. Examples of other forms of restriction that did indeed repress and strangle music will be brought forward in Chapter VIII.

(*b*) THE ESTABLISHED CHURCH

Puritanism is not the only manifestation of religion in the seventeenth century, even in reformed England. The Right wing of the English Church (such as was represented, for example, by the policy of Archbishop Laud) continued to delight in many forms of church music. What William Byrd (1543–1623) did for Roman Catholics in England, Thomas Weelkes (1576–1623), Orlando Gibbons (1583–1625), John Morley (1557–1603) and many others did for the Church of England. The art which appeared so felicitously in the madrigal-school was devoted to sacred music, and the result in Tudor and Early Stuart times was a noble treasury of sacred polyphony. English polyphony, if we except Byrd, is as different from the style of Palestrina as is Elgar from Brahms, but there is no doubt that the legacy of polyphony is a legacy shared equally between England and the Continent, between Anglican Protestantism and Roman Catholicism. In all this we have the continuing impetus which sixteenth century Europe gave to the composition of polyphony, and in it the church delighted. All European countries were at that time "musical"; music was a normal social accomplishment, and those Christians who believed rather in the integration of the Faith and common life than in their separation were content to see it in church, Englishmen adding the distinctive English quality to the technique they inherited from the Continent.

(c) THE NEW MUSIC

So free and facile is the flow of sacred polyphony all over Europe at the beginning of the seventeenth century that there seems no reason why it should ever have come to an end, had it not been for a development in Italy which changed the whole course of music. This was the operatic technique, which first appeared in the work of Giulio Caccini (1545–1618) and Jacopo Peri (1561–1633), to the second of whom belongs the distinction of having composed, in about 1600, the first opera. These composers used the human voice in a new way. In these works for the first time we see a solo voice, accompanied by instruments, singing an extended *aria*. We see, in fact, a "tune", which is to say that we have a new emphasis placed on a single part—often an upper part—at the expense of other parts. We have solo and accompaniment, or "tune" and "harmony", which is called in technical language the *monodic* style.

Subsequent musical history, especially English musical history, makes no sense until it is realised that this was an invention foreign to England. It led, by ways which we may not follow here, to the "European orthodoxy"[1] which distinguishes the

[1] This term is further explained in Chapter VIII, pp. 173–7.

tonality of all music from Bach to Brahms : in that
" orthodoxy " are implied the capacity in music for
conveying emotion, whether with or without the
help of words, the distinguishing of " subjects " or
fragmentary " tunes ", which is the secret of sonata
form, the acceptance of instrumental music as a form
not derivative from but transcending vocal music,
and an entirely new tradition of the solo or professional musician. In fact the operatic development
produced a new *kind* of music, which was neither
sacred nor secular in the sense that sixteenth-century
dances and madrigals were secular. It fitted neither
of these categories because it was so soon divorced
from language and, not much later, from dance-forms.[1]
It had to do with no specific human activity. It was a
new absolute language and for want of a better term
we shall have to call it what it is always popularly
called, " classical " music.

This was the Renaissance in music, delayed because
of the long association of music with words. The
church had had a monopoly of " serious " music for
fifteen centuries, but now it was neither the monopoly
of the church nor of the " world ". It was simply
music, and in the hands of the composers of the
eighteenth and nineteenth centuries it developed the
faculty for expressing connected thought and argument
in terms which are uniquely appropriate to the thought
and the argument. Beginning with a certain crude
humanism in the early opera, a new-found exuberance
of individual technique and melodic line, the new
music soon absorbed polyphony into itself and

[1] This transition from dance-forms to absolute forms is shown
in the transition in instrumental music from the suite to the symphony.

invaded the church. It invaded England as well, but England never completely assimilated the technique. English music was already so vital and original that for the highest developments of the classical style we look not to England but to the Continent ; hence also the fact that for its lowest perversions we look during the same period not to the Continent but to England.

(*d*) THE NEW MUSIC IN ENGLAND

It was the court of Charles II which introduced this new music to England on a large scale. When Charles came to the throne Giacomo Carissimi (1605–74) was composing his operas and cantatas in Italy, and the mighty Schutz (1585–1672) his " Passions " in Germany. In these composers and others of their kind the new humanism in music had a spectacular start on its long career, and it was early turned to the use of the church. But as we shall see, the relation between this new music and the church was soon shown to be a very different relation, even in the context of church-music, from that of the older music. In any case, Carissimi and Schutz are only representative examples of the highest that Continental music achieved in the seventeenth century. What Charles II had met on the Continent was the secular music, graceful but already showing signs of triviality. Above all things, this music was in a new way *tuneful*.

When he came to the throne this cultivated and unreliable monarch found English music by no means stagnant. The last generation of English polyphonists, James Shirley (1596–1666), Edward Coleman (d. 1669), Matthew Locke (c. 1632–77) and

Christopher Gibbons (1615–76), carried on the tradition of the madrigal school much as the later generations of Bachs carried on the tradition of the earlier—that is, writing with gracious competence but both with greater freedom of instrumentation and also with less compelling inspiration than their predecessors. Henry Lawes (1596–1662) was almost at the end of a life in which he had served the Reformed church well and earned the immortal admiration of John Milton. But the operatic tradition which the court of Charles brought with it broke over this peaceful scene like a metropolitan circus in an English village ; and it came, unlike the circus, to stay. The qualities of Italian and French music were first and best understood in England by John Blow (1648–1708), who passed on the tradition to his illustrious pupil, Purcell (1658–95).[1] The climax of this new music in England was certainly the operas in which Henry Purcell co-operated with John Dryden, and that greatest of his operas which he composed on his own, *Dido and Aeneas*.

But let it be remembered that these musicians and their contemporaries were primarily church musicians, choristers and organists who gave their services to the routine of the Church of England. Of these we may mention, for the sake of that most celebrated musical epigram, the " Grand Chant ",[2] Pelham Humfrey (1647–74), a chorister of the Chapel Royal

---

[1] The story of Blow's abdication from the organ-loft of Westminster Abbey in favour of his pupil and subsequent return to it on Purcell's untimely death is one of the happier stories in the annals of English music.

[2] This is the single chant on two notes commonly associated with Psalm 150.

who was sent to France by Charles II to learn the new music from the leading French composer, Lully, and to act thereafter as a channel through which England might be fertilised from France. The result of fertilisation was a new graciousness and tunefulness in English music, a pliancy or softness which the reader will find exemplified in the hymn-tunes of Jeremiah Clarke (1670–1707), especially those called *Uffingham*, *Bishopthorpe*, and *King's Norton*.[1]

This is the fertilisation not only of English by Continental music but of Protestant by Roman Catholic tradition, and any examination of the music of the first generation shows that it was to the advantage of the English and Protestant. And yet neither Englishry nor Protestantism are engulfed in the reaction of the Restoration. The music of Blow and Purcell and Clarke, though by no means Puritan in its genius, is as truly English as that of Vaughan Williams. The time had not yet come for England to give way completely to the Continental idiom. What we remark in Purcell at his best is a strength and solidity which well supports the imported gracefulness and delivers it from sentimentality. This is not only an English quality ; it is a quality of native English Protestantism—a firmness and independence which Purcell combined felicitously with the more compromising outlook of the Church of England of the Stuart dynasty.

On these developments the Church had little to say in a general way. Apart from the independent intensity of Puritanism in England and among the Continental Protestants, we find little sign of musical

[1] *Songs of Praise* (1931) 564, 536, and 547.

thought in the Western church ; and the truth is that the Western church on the Continent was too completely preoccupied with war and controversy to give much thought to such matters. The foreign policy of the Continental Catholic church was focussed for the first half of the century in the Thirty Years' War and in England the struggle between Puritan and Royalist up to the revolution of 1688 left little room for the kind of contemplation that produces musical criticism of the medieval sort. Therefore the seventeenth century is an age of undocumented evidences ; we find the effect of theology on music to be an unconscious and undetermined effect, and as such we have had to record it. We will now proceed to the eighteenth century and the strange developments that took place in music and theology as soon as James II and Henry Purcell were dead.

CHAPTER VII

THE EIGHTEENTH CENTURY

The Religious Temper in Europe—Theological Decadence and Musical Development—Church Music—Revival—Enlightenment.

(a) THE RELIGIOUS TEMPER IN EUROPE

Both in England and on the Continent the whole atmosphere of the eighteenth century is conditioned by the fact that religious wars had ceased. The religious temper of that age was the temper of a community which had been for many generations a fighting community, and, now that the fighting was done, had to discover afresh what besides fighting was worth living for. This is true equally of Protestant and Catholic, of English and Continental communities. The eighteenth century opens on a " peace " as dangerous as the periods of " peace " which followed the two twentieth century world wars. This fact is, of course, most important for our study. Evidences of it are numerous, and we need only mention a few.

Consider the transformation of English Puritanism. That theology which was founded in the sovereignty of God (the theology of John Calvin), now no longer embattled, softened into Unitarianism and Arianism, and those who had fought for the " Crown rights of the Redeemer" now fought in controversy over the doctrine of the Trinity. Arianism had a short but by no means negligible vogue in this country in the early decades of the eighteenth century, and the biography, for example, of Isaac Watts[1](1674–1748) indicates the temper of the controversy and the insidious way in which the Arian heresy could find hospitality (though only momentarily) in such a mind as Watts' own. Again, Puritan politics were, as expounded by John Calvin and his English followers Browne, Greenwood, and to some extent Hooker, the politics of Christian democracy, the sanctification of the new doctrine of the importance of the individual. But the Independent and Baptist churches of, say, 1725,[2] were beginning to lose their democratic qualities : in the towns (though not for a long time in the countryside) they began to settle down as churches of the business class. Far more than at present, the heirs of Puritanism lent their aid to the progressive stratification of society which marks the social history of this century. Again, it was during this century that Puritan morality became " puritanical " ; by reference to the work of such preachers as Jonathan Edwards (1703–58) Dr. Scholes shows[3] how the conception which identified the words " worldly " and " abandoned " gained ground during this time.

The same symptoms are apparent on the Continent. After the Thirty Years' War, in which both sides suffered grievously, but in which the heavier losses were on the side of the Protestants, neither Roman nor Protestant returned to the ideals of the sixteenth century. In Protestantism we find little of the

---

[1] A. P. Davis, *Isaac Watts* (Independent Press, 1948).

[2] Davis, op. cit. ch. II, for a description of Watts's own church in Mark Lane, London.

[3] *The Puritans and Music*, pp. 356 ff.

primitive passion of Luther or the discipline of Calvin, nor in the Catholics do we see, apart from the isolated example here and there, much of the spirit of the Council of Trent. In France, for example, that democracy which as a result of Huguenot influence had gained ground during the sixteenth century received a set-back, and the court life which was revived under Louis XIV coupled with the irreparable weakening of the church's hold on politics led to that corruption for which the only cure was the slaughter and atheism of the French Revolution.

In the eighteenth century, therefore, we may expect to find evidences of a degenerate traditionalism, of religious revival, and of pagan reaction. All three movements are the natural result of the apathy which everhung the Europe of the early eighteenth century.

(*b*) THEOLOGICAL DECADENCE AND MUSICAL DEVELOPMENT

We have already referred to the mild Calvinism of Protestant England which turned in many cases to a form of Unitarianism. Of the same kind, considered historically, was that German Pietism which, being an intensely individual piety without any " fighting " qualities of doctrine, bore the same relation to the Evangelical teaching of Luther that contemporary English Calvinism bore to the teaching of Calvin ; this, at all events, until the remarkable energy of Zinzendorf (1700–60) turned Pietism into a Revival by bringing to it something of the primitive fire of his hero, John Hus. The language of Pietism can be seen very well in the words of most of the Bach Cantatas and these devotional exercises fall upon modern ears with an almost repulsive effect if they are divorced from the music that has immortalised them. And even when Zinzendorf brought to Pietism his evangelical zeal, it became a revival not of the church but of individuals. The immense outpouring of "spiritual songs" designed for individual or family use, not for congregational singing, which Zinzendorf and his friends compassed, was typical of the activity of the new Moravianism. There was nothing here remotely resembling the *democratic* aspects of the Renaissance ; this form of piety was exactly complementary to and exclusive of Puritan churchmanship.

(*c*) CHURCH MUSIC

These then are two examples of many which could be furnished of the background-religion of eighteenth century Europe. The Roman Catholic church undergoes exactly the same change from the energy and fighting evangelism of the sixteenth-century Jesuits to the more or less comfortable court and peasant religion of France, Spain, and Italy. This condition of things had the effect on church music of allowing music to take its own course without interference of any kind. Toleration was the order of the day, and the new dramatic possibilities of music which the seventeenth century had already foreshadowed were welcomed by the church at large as an enrichment of the liturgy. Only the Puritans stood aloof. Independents, Baptists and Presbyterians continued to sing their psalm-versions and the hymns of Isaac Watts—though perhaps with less heartiness and zeal than had their fathers (Isaac Watts's famous Preface to his *Hymns and Spiritual Songs* indicates how ill in this respect the church of 1707 was adapting itself to the disciplines of peace) ; but in the Continental church, both in the German and Latin countries, we find a great output of masses, cantatas, and other liturgical or extra-liturgical music by musicians who genuinely strove to offer to the Church the best that their new art could provide. Indeed, it was not only music in the " new style " that was thus offered to the church ; not only the pomp of Marcello's *Psalms* (1724) and the majesty of the *Stabat Mater* of Pergolesi (1710–36), but the severe *a cappella* style of Palotta (1680–1758) and Pisari (1725–78) appear in the church music of the Continent. In Germany Johann Joseph Fux (1660–1741) leads the school of quasi-operatic cantata-composers in the Catholic church, and his work exemplifies admirably the style of truly Christian baroque.

This is the main stream of liturgical church music as seen in the Roman Catholic church ; but on both sides of it can be seen divergences of which we must take note. The most remarkable phenomenon of the eighteenth century is the appearance of church-music on the scale of Bach's *Mass in B minor*. The difference between this and the church-music which we mentioned in the last paragraph is that it is liturgical in origin but not in fact. The *Mass in B minor* could not, in fact, be part of a Celebration in the way in which the Masses of Byrd could. It stands in its own right, not in the kingdom of church music but in this new category of "classical music". And further, it is the work of a Protestant, in whose Lutheran tradition the Mass in its full text has no place at all. Here, surely, is renewed justification for our comment in an earlier chapter that we have in these centuries a Church that is divided and yet still a Church. From what did Bach derive this work, and to what was he offering it ? The answer is—Christendom, or the Universal Church, or the Invisible Church, the inheritor and custodian of Christian belief, which transcends the denominations and schisms. To this same category belong the *Passions* of Bach and, despite the fact that it was commissioned for an actual celebration, the *Mass in D* of Beethoven. Now that music has come to its full stature as an independent language, an independent medium for thought, Christians lose no time in making it a medium of Christian thought. The *Mass in B Minor* is as ecumenical a gesture as the World Council of Churches.

On the other side of the main stream of church music we find the music of the Church of England of the eighteenth century, as represented by such composers as Maurice Greene (1695–1755), William Hayes (1706–77), Benjamin Cooke (1730–93), William Boyce (1710–79), and Samuel Wesley (1766–1837).[1] In this music we find a restraint and sobriety which is remarkable when it is contrasted with the church music of the Continent. It is only in its wider scope and its use of instruments and harmony that it differs from the music of the Puritan inheritance. The reason for this is, at the least, twofold. First, the English composers were handling a new idiom and a foreign idiom. Their music, especially their church music, retains its English quality in its very

[1] Wesley is obviously to be included here, in as much as all his important music was composed before he suffered a serious accident in his twenty-first year.

simplicity, but in its abandonment of all modal tonality and its largely homophonic character it follows the lead of the continental schools. It is only the occasional movement or episode that is in contrapuntal form in the English music of this time, and there is a courtly formality about the whole which suggests that the new language and thought forms are being accepted with reserve. These composers were unable to use the new idiom with the freedom of a John Sebastian Bach or with the abandon and lightness of his immediate heirs. This is not to say that English music of the eighteenth century is a pale imitation of the continental. It is the continental idiom spoken by Englishmen, as Englishmen always speak continental languages, with a strong English accent. There is here no collision between music and the church, not merely because the Church for which it was written was disinclined to criticise but also because of the singular blamelessness of the music itself. But it is worth noting, as a strand of history which we shall pick up again, that it is in their church music that the English musicians of the eighteenth century made their most distinctive, in fact their most English, contribution to European music.

(*d*) REVIVAL

Now we may turn to the second manifestation of religious history in the eighteenth century—the Revival ; and here we shall be dealing, of course, in chief with the Wesleyan revival. It is worth observing at once that the Wesleyan Revival was not only the first of many Revivals, but was unique among them all in being far more than a local and emotional and transient movement. John Wesley himself remained a member of the Church of England and regarded all occasions of dissension between himself and his church as matters for great sorrow. He was no schismatic. On the contrary he was a singularly orthodox and careful theologian. As a preacher he relied not at all upon histrionic gifts, if what we read of him is true. His power lay not in his external gifts or in any devices of display but in the content of his thought and speech. Like all revivalists he was a fighter, but he did not, like most others, rely primarily for his message on the denunciation of abuses. He relied on an ancient Gospel of power, wrath, and mercy.

He had made contact with Zinzendorf while they were both in their thirties, and had gathered from him the power of evangelisation through song. But the Wesleyan evangelism was of a very different order from that of Zinzendorf. True, it was individual rather than high-churchly ; but it was severely and comprehensively theological : a few pages of Charles Wesley's seven thousand hymns give sufficient evidence of that. Wesley's own views on music were those of the theologian who knows the principles without having specialised knowledge. He knew what *sort* of music was fit to use, even if he committed himself to no dogmatism on the matter.

The musical editions of the early Methodist hymn-books show how closely the Wesleyans kept in their early days to the traditional theories of religious music current in England. But the tradition they followed was not that of the Puritans but that of the Anglicans. The distinguishing mark of early Methodist tunes is

" tunefulness ", which they gather from the operatic tradition of the continent by way of Purcell (whose music Wesley greatly admired) and Jeremiah Clarke. The suave and sequential melody of the tune to which we have already referred, *Bishopthorpe*, the pastoral peacefulness of Henry Carey's *Surrey*,[1] and the free-moving facility of Purcell's " Fairest Isle " are the direct ancestors of early Methodist hymnody. The many musical editions of Methodist and Methodist-derived hymn-books in the eighteenth century show a large number of these tuneful, triple-time melodies full of those ornaments and apoggiaturas which suggest irstrumental traditions, some of them derived from secular sources, but most of them composed especially by anonymous musicians, and the standard which they maintain is, in the earlier years, high. If the reader reaches for his hymnal and turns to the tunes *University*,[2] *Helmsley*[3] (which is of secular origin), and *Irish*[4] he will find early Methodist hymnody at its best. And if he turns to *Easter Hymn*[5] in its modern version (altered by the Wesleyans), to *Kent*[6] (*Devonshire*) and to *Leoni*[7] (a Jewish tune brought into currency by Wesleyans) he will see that these same revivalists did not turn their backs on the strong and even austere.

But all revivals stand in great danger. They call

[1] S.P. 656.
[2] S.P. 653.
[3] S.P. 65.
[4] S.P. 680.
[5] S.P. 145.
[6] S.P. 524.
[7] S.P. 398.

out the fighting spirit in their leaders and adherents, and that fighting spirit often consorts ill with recollected thought. Moreover the fighting spirit, when its first enemies are conquered, tends to look for more enemies, and thereby to become more destructive than constructive. It is the mark of failing energy in a Revival when its leaders turn on one another and when its message is one of denunciation rather than of hope. And it is about the time when this phase came upon Methodism that we find the sad degeneration of Methodist hymnody, the intrusion of "fugal" hymn-tunes, the too-facile melody and the poverty-stricken harmony. This consideration, however, takes us into the nineteenth century and we will deal with it in the next chapter.

It is enough to say here that the implicit Methodist doctrine of hymnody seems to be this : Give us the best music we can have, but make it *friendly* to the people. Therefore Methodist hymnody entirely subserves the musical spirit of the age, the monodic and tuneful texture, the insistence on the major mode, the suggestion of instrumentation in florid melody, the sequential and stepwise-moving tune that easily "takes" at the first time of singing. Wesleyan hymnody was "music for the people", it was the return of democracy to church-music, and it was more democratic than Calvin or even Luther because in proportion as its more hospitable theology admitted the capacity of all things for redemption it was able to make greater use of the secular idiom. But it shared with the universal church the conviction that music acts upon the singer with an effect corresponding in benefit to the integrity of the music.

(e) " ENLIGHTENMENT "

The third phase of the eighteenth century which bears on this study is the " Enlightenment ", which was the answer of the sceptic and the critic to the religious apathy of the age, just as Revival was the answer of the religiously zealous. Like " Renaissance " " Enlightenment " is a word covering a large number of different activities ; it describes a world-view which affected politics, philosophy, art, and religion. It was directly responsible for the Romantic movement in those same spheres, and is to be seen in the new respect for Nature and Men as natural phenomena which far outdoes the Renaissance in its violence. The Renaissance was always Christian, but Enlightenment questioned Christianity ; Christianity was one of those forces which seemed to prevent man from being (in the sense in which Rousseau used the word) " free ", and therefore Christianity had to be questioned. In one phase, in fact, a determined attempt was made to uproot all its institutions.

Into all this we may not enter now. The importance of the Enlightenment for our present purposes is the fact that whereas for two hundred years men had been seeking and tasting a kind of freedom which was unknown, and largely undesired, in the Middle Ages—the freedom of controlling their own destiny— the Enlightenment gave men political, philosophical, and eventually religious justifications for all they had fought to win in the seventeenth century, all that of which the reaction of the eighteenth century had threatened to deprive them. The fact that this produced Rationalism here and Liberalism there bears only indirectly on our thesis. Even its effects on the church had no noticeable reflections in church music. But in the liberation of imagination, the reaction against the formal and artificial, which marked all forms of art under the Romantic movement, music took on a new richness of vocabulary, a wider sweep of reference, which was all that was required to make Beethoven possible.

But the important point to be made here about the Enlightenment is that under the influence of this movement the future course of the " new music " was directed away from the church. Despite the loosening effect of the Renaissance and the disciplines of the Reformation, both of which in their way had done a good deal to undermine the presupposition that art was primarily a religious phenomenon and was at its best only when it was overtly serving the church, there was still in many quarters a lingering feeling that although the new art of the Renaissance was not subject in its details to the dictates of ecclesiastics, yet art still served its best purpose when it served the church. Immediately before the Enlightenment there had been, as we have already observed, some reaction towards the medieval hierarchical culture in certain European countries, and this only made the more violent the new conception of the real autonomy of art. It might be said that in the thirteenth century art was a dependency of the Church, in the sixteenth a self-governing but loyal dominion, and by 1800 an autonomous sovereign state with its own currency and its own immigration laws. It would be wrong to say that art became " secularised ", since the proper meaning of that word is "controlled not by the church but by the State". Neither in the Middle Ages nor in the eighteenth century is there any question of control. In the Middle Ages it was a question of accepted obedience, now of independence. The artist under the Romantic influence began to spell himself with a capital A and to say, not without stridency, that he took orders from nobody. Thus absolute music becomes "absolute" in a new sense ; not only is it free from the associations of words and dance-forms, but it is free from any connection with the institutions of Church or of Court.

CHAPTER VIII

THE NINETEENTH CENTURY

THE purpose of this chapter will be to offer some explanation and some comment relevant to that decadence in church music for which the nineteenth century has become notorious. What is offered here presupposes that any criticism of that music which ignores the spiritual and theological categories can get no further than the technique of reaction and counter-reaction which so clearly characterises what the twentieth century has said up to now concerning the nineteenth. The Christian categories with which we have by now become familiar will throw much-needed light on this strange problem, and the problem in its turn will give us guidance upon the contemporary application of the categories.

The nineteenth century, partly because of its nearness to our own in time, presents an aspect more complex and baffling than any of its predecessors, and any attempt to generalise about it within the compass of a chapter will necessarily be guilty of artificial simplification. The least misleading way in which to present the problem of the nineteenth century as it concerns this study is to describe the century under a threefold label. We will say that it is the Age of Success, the Age of Tools, and the Age of Exile.

(a) THE AGE OF SUCCESS

The most spectacular characteristic of the nineteenth century is, of course, the success with which man's dominion over his environment asserted itself. Scientific invention leapt forward from James Watt to Marconi ; the Industrial Revolution was made possible by the subjugation by man of nature through the machine. The Empire of Britain, well founded in the eighteenth century, continued to expand and prosper. The Church extended its boundaries to the ends of the earth as the result of the work of missionary societies of which the first, the Baptist Missionary Society, was founded in 1792.[1]

Whatever man did in the scientific and commercial worlds seemed to prosper, and the natural result of this in the worlds of thought and even of theology was a doctrine of evolution (which we associate with the publication in 1859 of Darwin's *Origin of Species*) and of progress towards a material heaven. The enormous buildings which the nonconformists erected during the latter half of the century, the inutility of which is only matched by their hideousness, are the fruit of this boundless confidence that progress would continue in the church in the shape of infinitely and inevitably increasing congregations. Bigger and better business reflected itself in bigger and more imposing ecclesiastical schemes and, indeed, in bigger and more impressive ecclesiastical demeanours, voices, sermons, and books.[2]

---

[1] See K. S. Latourette, *History of the Expansion of Christianity* vol. IV, chs. 1-4.

[2] In this connection we may mention *The Second Evangelical Awakening* by Edmund Orr (1949), whose thesis is that about the year 1859 England and America were swept by a religious revival comparable to that associated with the Wesleys. The curious story told there confirms the opinion that " religious success " was one of the keynotes of the nineteenth century.

The Nineteenth Century

All this was made possible by an important discovery which mankind in the West seems to have made
just before the beginning of the nineteenth century—
the discovery of the possibilities of the machine.
This, to serve our purpose, is better described as the
discovery of tools, and referred to the philosophical
category of means and ends. For the discovery of
tools is the discovery of the results man can obtain by
using a thing for an end which may not be intrinsically
its own. Aristotle held, it will be recalled, that everything has its own " end " or " function ", the proper
performance of which is the measure of its goodness.
Nineteenth century commercial man found the strange
secret of judging things not by the fulfilment of their
own ends but by the fulfilment of some end which is
ordained by man.

No doubt the origin of this is to be found in the
modern associations of money, which had been growing up ever since the Reformation and had been
established by the foundation of the Bank of England
in 1694. Money is, of course, a pivotal example of a
commodity which has in itself no end and only fulfils
what Aristotle called its " function " in being a means
to some end in which it has itself no part. The process
by which the legitimate use of money developed into
an idolatry is the archetype of the degeneration which
overtook every civilised activity during the nineteenth
century. The machines which give their name to the
age, being themselves a whole class of objects which
exist not for themselves but only " to be used ", are as
certainly derived from the new mythology of money

as they are the cause of the Forsytean refusal to assess any object otherwise than by the measure of " what it will fetch ".

Now this attitude of assuming that everything exists " to be used " is the direct denial of Greek and also of Biblical pilosophy. The reverence inseparable from *theoria*[1] is precisely what the nineteenth century allowed to be dissipated. The Biblical teaching that nature was man's dominion and also his responsibility was now distorted into the doctrine that everything exists in order that man may make as much for himself out of it as he can. In as much as this philosophy informed the enterprise and the crude fortitude of men, it armed them serviceably for war against those things upon which he could legitimately make war. The dominion of disease, for example, being a province of the dominion of evil, demanded from men direct and drastic attack, and this to the lasting benefit of humanity it received ; the triumph of science over suffering is the great and shining light of the nineteenth century. But when man came to regard as legitimate fields of conquest, exploitation and loot whole areas which a thousand generations had not even thought of as enemy territory, mischief was done. The very age which abolished the fear of plague invented a score of new occupational diseases. The soil, for a thousand years the livelihood of Englishmen, was alternately neglected and bullied into a resentful subjection with the consequences of which the modern miner and farmer are hard pressed to deal. Men were enslaved on an unparalleled scale, and experienced that most terrible of newly-invented diseases, the disease

[1] See page 18.

technically called " redundancy " which is " being unwanted ", or more strictly, " being of no *use* ".

Even this describes only the foreground of the picture. The characteristic quality of the nineteenth-century mind must be described as impatience with the " thing in itself ",and this impatience is reflected in all the intolerance of authority, discipline, reverence, contemplation, and leisure, all the corresponding exaltation of haste, efficiency, abruptness, and ruthlessness which is the fabric of industrial society and which the true heir of the Middle Ages, the Irishman or the Latin peasant, derides and hates with such passion. Not all the fruits of this impatient mind were evil, for it was not this mind which invented evil ; but neither was any of its fruits unmixed with bitterness. The political notion of Freedom, secularised and transformed by Voltaire, brought with it the French Revolution, upon which it is becoming much more difficult than it was once thought to be to make a simple historical judgment. Intellectual impatience issued in the anarchy of scepticism, some of it honest doubt, some of it a new superstition. The supernatural and metaphysical in religion and theology took second place to the practical ; the subjectivism of Friedrich Schleiermacher,[1] the moralism of Albrecht Ritschl,[2] the dialectic of Hegel,[3] all have in common a flight from Kant's[4] uncompromising objectivism to the subjective and practical. Much good came of the researches of these good men, but Schleiermacher cannot claim to have no share in the sentimentality of much nineteenth-century religious thought, nor

[1] 1768–1834.   [2] 1822–1889.
[3] *Philosophie des Rechts,* 1821.
[4] 1740–1824.

169

Ritschl in its offensive pseudo-Puritan moralism, nor Hegel in the political nightmare of Marx.

The English Christians of the nineteenth century are at their most powerful and influential in their social and reforming work, in which great and deserved honour is given to F. D. Maurice, Charles Kingsley, Lord Shaftesbury and Elizabeth Fry among many others ; but their scholarly and metaphysical work tended more and more to the critical and even destructive work which, itself not without great importance in the evolution of Biblical theology, could not be brought to its proper fruit without the new reverence and patience of the twentieth century school of Biblical theologians. Finally Romanticism, the aesthetic fruit of the impatience of the eighteenth century, gives perhaps the most compendious example of the temper of the nineteenth century in spiritual matters ; for of Romanticism were brought forth twin fruits, corresponding almost exactly to penitence and pride ; on the one hand, men found a new conviction of their own smallness, a new faculty of admiration and imagination, a new sense of wonder and adventure, and on the other, they conceived the sinister image of the *Übermensch*, the hideous idolatry of " blood and soil ", the worship of power, the cultivation of the titanic.[1]

All these manifestations spring from the same root —a fundamental contempt for things as they are which makes one man see them smaller and his neighbour greater than life-size. The man who sees

[1] For an analysis of Romanticism which singularly combines brevity with completeness, see the opening pages of the Preface to the third (enlarged) edition of C. S. Lewis's *The Pilgrim's Regress* (1943).

them magnified delivers himself up a joyful sacrifice
to the man who sees them diminished, and the result
is power-politics, dictatorship, and all those ex-
ploitations of the collective mind which are so typical of
the age of individualism.

The truth, then, about the Age of Tools can be thus
summarised. As a result of man's rebellion against
the discipline of seeing things as they are, and his insistence upon determining for himself the manner
in which he will see them, the relation between men
and things, and between men and men, instead of
being simplified, is confused. The result of this
confusion is the inextricable complexity of modern
thought and modern society ; that complexity is the
anchylosis which is the inevitable consequence of the
dislocation of delicate ligaments of courtesy and
muscles of obligation in the body of politics and of
philosophy. At the root of it is no single action, no
historical event, but a corporate act of rebellion against
the commonplaceness of things, of which commonplaceness the artificial society of the eighteenth century
had fashioned a prison. The reality of the sin that
had made this rebellion necessary, however, does not
in any way affect the judgment which must be made on
it, that it was seriously affected by what St. Augustine,
in a passage we have already attended to, called both
amor agendi (the love of *doing*) and *superbia* (pride).[1]

(c) THE AGE OF EXILE

Returning to the immediate foreground of the
picture which we are forming of the nineteenth century

[1] The whole question of ignoring final causes is carried much further
than this in C. S. Lewis's *The Abolition of Man* (1943), Section 3, q.v.

we have to add to our descriptions of it as the age of success and the age of tools that it was the age of exile ; by this we mean that for by far the greater part of the population of England, the nineteenth century was a time of homelessness.

The conquest of the world which England achieved during this century was accompanied by the dispossession of a whole section of the population. Ever since the social upheavals of the sixteenth century had put an end to feudal society the peasantry of England had been gradually losing their honour and their vocation ; but it was only with the industrial revolution that they began actually to leave the land for the city. For the rude discipline of the earth the new industrial city offered the hazardous dream of quick wealth. The manufacturers tempted the peasantry from the fields to the streets, and the result was the industrial cities of England. The new civilisation gave the peasantry a new experience of insecurity. Formerly their enemies were disease, the weather, and the harsh landlord ; but these were tangible and, one might almost say, predictable things compared with the new enemy, which was unemployment and starvation. Even if it be admitted that few things could be meaner than the lot of the eighteenth century English peasant, among those things must surely be included the lot of the nineteenth century industrial peasant, and the difference between the new meanness and the old is the difference between that which is produced directly by man's conflict with nature and his own elemental sins, and that which is produced by these things at several removes. The unbelievable loneliness of the tenement-dwellers, of which any London missioner can tell to-day, the solitariness and despair which can engulf those who dwell in the mighty cliff-dwellings of the East End of London among five thousand neighbours—this is the result of the dispossession of the population. In our industrial cities men not only do not own or work on any land ; they often do not even live on the ground, but four or five stories above it.

The result of this new insecurity is to be seen in both the dispossessed and the possessing. The possessing, being mostly people of excellent intention who were greatly shocked by the monstrous consequences of the industrial society they had helped to create, turned either to active philanthropy or to that form of religious discipline which would the most readily justify the security which they had hardly won and which they precariously retained at the expense of their neighbours. The dispossessed were concerned entirely with finding a home.

We mention this in order to place the music of the nineteenth century against its background. The rest of the chapter will be devoted to proving that this analysis provides the clues to a proper understanding of the phenomenon of nineteenth century Bad Music. Bad composition, we shall argue, was the result of the Age of Tools, degenerate appreciation that of the Age of Exile.

(d) THE RHETORICAL DEVELOPMENT OF MUSIC

The single word " rhetoric " sums up the direction of the development of nineteenth-century music, and its uses as a category can be supported by the following facts :

1. The music of the Romantics, that is, of Beethoven and his successors, is notable for a spectacularly increased musical vocabulary which is particularly developed in the direction of evoking and expressing human emotion.

2. The new expressiveness of this music, exploited in different ways by such highly individual composers as Chopin, Liszt, Wagner, and Brahms, is not greater in degree than the expressiveness of the classical music (e.g., J. S. Bach), but is achieved by devices which are more easily detected as devices and can be more easily isolated by the listener.

3. The word " concert " in the eighteenth century meant a group of instrumentalists playing together, but in the nineteenth century it means a group of instrumentalists playing *to an audience*.

4. The practice of orchestral conducting, which made possible the great size, complexity, and expressiveness of the modern orchestra, dates from the second half of the eighteenth century.

The background of these phenomena in history can be briefly sketched in the following summary of musical development from 1600.

It will be recalled that music took a very important turn at the advent of the Italian operatic style in the works of Peri and Caccini. This development was, superficially, a new emphasis on melody, which involved in music a new " class-distinction " between melody and accompaniment ; this distinction was soon reflected in the distinction in musical society between the virtuoso and the rank-and-file musician, or, later, between the professional and the amateur.

The Nineteenth Century

Three important musical corollaries accompany this vital change in musical thought-form.

First, the technique of counterpoint is thrust into the background of music. This is not to say that counterpoint is abolished in favour of harmony or monody, for there can be no harmony which does not involve the counterpoint of two or more voices singing together. But counterpoint, which occupied the foreground in the music of the sixteenth century, was in the new music an integral but less obtrusive part of the music's structure. The only composer in the eighteenth and nineteenth centuries to give any great proportion of his time to compositions in pure polyphony was J. S. Bach ; on the other hand, Brahms, who wrote scarcely a single fugue otherwise than by way of exercise, wrote all his music with the strictest attention to counterpoint, and indeed many of his pages which strike the listener at first hearing as purely melodic are in fact written in triple counterpoint.[1] But it did become possible for the superficial listener to think of music as plain " melody and bass ".

Secondly, the new emphasis on melody made possible the building up of music, by the use of contrasting themes and the technique of " development ", into a connected argument of a kind for which pure polyphony had not up to that time given scope. For while the argument of sixteenth century polyphony consisted in the polyphony itself and extended only over a very short space of time, the argument in a sonata movement could be spread over twenty minutes

[1] The most familiar example of this is the fourth variation in the *Variations on a Theme of Haydn,* which is written throughout in strict triple counterpoint.

or more, and in a Wagner opera over several hours. In fact the argument of ancient polyphony was "argument" in the ancient sense of terse, precise statement, while that of the new music was "argument" in the modern sense of discussion and the clash of contrasting issues.

Thirdly, the new music had an effect on *tonality* which should not be overlooked. This was to polarise music on an outer axis of "major and minor" modes and an inner axis of "tonic and dominant". That is, the ecclesiastical modes disappeared and were replaced by the classical scales and key-relationships. Beyond this we cannot go now, but we must observe that in both these axes there is an element of tension, or unstable equilibrium. It is obvious that on the inner axis the tension is away from the dominant towards the tonic ; the naturalness of the perfect cadence (the movement of the bass from the fifth of the scale to the keynote) as a close to the simplest musical phrase is proof of this. But similarly the presupposition is from the beginning that "major" is normal and "minor" abnormal. This point is proved if it be recalled how very few works in symphonic style (that is, written in several movements which observe internally and in relation to each other the principles of key-relationship) have all their movements, and how few single movements have all their subjects, in the minor mode.

In this way was built up a "European orthodoxy" which, as we have already hinted, found its way into England through the court-society of the eighteenth century. This society, stratified to an exaggerated degree, encouraged just the virtuosity and professional-

ism in which the continental music flourished, and by
the same token it discouraged and all but drove out of
existence the essentially amateur and homespun style
of English folk-music. English folk-song went
underground so completely that it has required a
team of professional archaeologists to disinter the
people's song.

(*e*) MUSIC AS A TOOL

Let it be fully conceded that during the nineteenth
century music rose to heights which it had itself never
surpassed in its history, and to which no other art in
that century came near. This fact needs here only
this comment, that the rhetorical technique happened
to suit the genius of music at this point in its development more completely than it suited the genius of the
other and (in respect of development) older arts ;
and it requires this limitation, that the zenith of music
to which we refer was achieved in the German
countries, only to a far less degree in the Latin
countries, and not at all in our own.

But there is another side to the picture. During the
nineteenth century in Europe music was not un-
touched by the virus of " tool-making " whose effect
on other areas of life we have already observed. It
became, during that time, a means of livelihood for
performers, composers, and (far more) publishers
and impresarios. In another plane, it became a
creator of " atmosphere ", a means of acting upon a
mass of men collectively, a seal of social standing for
young ladies of quality ; in the hands of some it
became a "means of self-expression", and it could
carry a " programme " of non-musical ideas. Upon

this we make two comments ; first, that this kind of
degeneracy attacked music in the countries of Europe
in inverse ratio to the nearness of that country to the
centre of musical development,—that is, we see it at
its most serious in England and at its least in Vienna ;
and second, that in England, where we see the worst of
it, this degeneracy is especially welcomed and even
fostered by the church.

That is the general proposition—that the use of
music as a " tool " is well established in the nineteenth
century. A few examples of this will suffice. Consider first the more blameless examples of the movement. The music of Franz Liszt (1811–86) remains
an enigma to the critics because of the association
which the composer establishes between so much of it
and pictorial, mythical, or otherwise non-musical
ideas. In a way essentially different from the
Pastoral Symphony of Beethoven and even the patriotic
music of Chopin, the music of Liszt at its best (for
example in the *Années de Pélerinage*) is pictorial ; but
at its best it is also excellent music. His imitators,
however, sought to achieve the pictorial effect of
Rustling Leaves or any other similar subject of romantic
imagery without any pretension to musical integrity,
with the result that their music could not be, as
Liszt's was, the object of *theoria*, a thing to be enjoyed
and admired in itself, but could only be used as a
means of conjuring up the " atmosphere " of spring-
time in a well-sealed suburban drawing-room. This
is music used as a " tool " ; Liszt's is not, at its best,
" tool-music ", but the romanticisms of his imitators
were precisely that.

Again, the music of the Romantic composers was,

as we have said, a singularly powerful transmitter of strong emotion.

The use of discord, chromatic harmony and, well-marked rhythms was its special technique. Chromatic harmony to express high emotional tension is as old as Palestrina's *Stabat Mater*, and some astonishing examples of it are to be found in, for example, the work of Carlo Gesualdo (1557–1630).[1] Bach used it with most moving effect in the *Passions*, Cantatas, and especially in the choral preludes for organ. Beethoven added to harmony rhythmical power, as in the Fifth Symphony and (using the same device) several other works of the same period. The power of Chopin's Polonaises, which are the fruits of his greatest passion, is not only in their haunting harmony but also in their almost hypnotic rhythm (which is, after all, only in detail different from that of the Bolero, a rhythm made celebrated by Ravel). All this was clear to the nineteenth-century musician of less accomplishment than the masters ; and the new facility of publishing and collecting audiences tempted him to produce second-rate music whose second-rateness consisted precisely in being second-hand, in imitating the external elements of the masters without attempting to compass their metaphysical integrity. The vice of Victorian music is often said to be " sentimentality ", and if sentimentality is emotional content backed by no solid truth, a show of feeling with no intention of consequent honesty, the description is an accurate

---

[1] For some striking quotations from this composer, see **exx.** 196–8 in R. O. Morris's *Contrapuntal Technique* (Oxford, 1922), and for an account of his life, the final essay in Cecil Gray's *Contingencies* (Oxford, 1947).

one. Hence, at any rate, came the multitudinous drawing-room and salon music of the later Victorian era, and this music was " tool-music " at two levels : it was music composed and published in order to help the business of music-making along, and in that sense a tool ; and it was music composed in order to create irresponsible emotion and an unreal sense of well-being, and in that sense also a tool.

But this music, the secular music of the salon, was not the final degradation. It remained for the church to debase music to the limit. For music designed to create mere natural emotions such as sorrow or pity, or peace of mind has at any rate what a celebrated broadcaster calls " animal content ". But the hack-music of the church, of which our hymnals are still full, and which our churches are only now beginning to abandon, music designed to produce not natural emotion but (save the mark) religious emotion —this was music at its lowest ebb.

Victorian church music, which we shall take as the example of this generalisation, can be described as music which occasionally rises to greatness, often achieves a serviceable character, but which is prone to diverge from even the serviceable ideal in the directions either of supreme tedium or of shameless vulgarity. The best English musicians of the century were perhaps John Goss (1800–80), Henry Smart (1813–79), Thomas Attwood. Walmisley (1814–56), Frederick Arthur Gore Ouseley (1825–89), Samuel Sebastian Wesley (1810–76) and John Stainer (1840–1901). Of these Walmisley probably maintained the soundest

---

[1] See the chapter in E. H. Fellowes' *English Cathedral Music* on " The Victorians ", for an excellent summary of this period.

general level, Wesley was capable of the highest flights (as in *The Wilderness*) and Smart was the least capable of either greatness or indiscretion.

Those musicians who drew on classical rather than romantic music for their models tended to produce workmanlike music sometimes of surpassing dullness and sometimes, like Walmisley's *Service in D minor*, or Attwood's *Come, Holy Ghost*, of real inspiration. Those who follow the Romantics were in worse case, for they had their musical tradition from the Romantic school through that of French and Italian opera and the music of the continental Roman Catholic church. The influence of Ludwig Spohr and Charles Gounod on English Church music was to cause our composers (for example, Arthur Sullivan, John Stainer, and John Bacchus Dykes) to abandon all contrapuntal and harmonic integrity in favour of a musical sensationalism which transgresses the bounds of good taste with dreary regularity. (See, for example, Sullivan's anthems *I will mention* and *Sing, O heavens*, Stainer's *Crucifixion*, Sullivan's *Festival Te Deum*, and Maunder's *Olivet to Calvary*, which last work perhaps achieved the highest index of combined popularity and banality). If, indeed, the church music of Sir Arthur Sullivan be set beside the magical felicity of his Savoy operas, the degeneracy of " tool-music " will be seen happily symbolised. For such music does admirably well for the light opera : indeed, in the process of his facile and inspired composition for the Savoy operas Sullivan achieved more than one great moment ; this is " tool-music " at its most innocent. But Sullivan's idea of " catching the atmosphere " of public worship as it is given to us in the *Te Deum* is clearly as unreal and sentimental as his fantasies of the Savoy Theatre were solid and sane.

Perhaps a fairer source for the folk-music of the religious bourgeoisie of England is not the music of the cathedral, to which we have referred, but that of the parish-church, which we find epitomised in *Hymns Ancient and Modern*. In the first three editions of this book the rake's progress of English church music is dramatically set forth. The hero of the tale is John Bacchus Dykes (1823–76), of whose hymn-tunes seven (his seven best, oddly enough) appear in the first edition (1861, 273 hymns), and fifty-seven in the third (1875, 473 hymns). This composer, whose place in English hymnody is honoured for one magnificent tune,[1] is quintessentially Victorian in his methods. Except in the one great tune, which draws on the common coin of sixteenth-century hymnody as it was minted in *Wachet Auf*, he gathers his material from the continental opera, and every one of his tunes shows a combination of seductive melody with a clearly discernible structural failure.[2] The affinity between more than one of his phrases and the general temper of Liszt's *Liebesträume* is clear enough[3] to strike the most casual hearer. It is obvious that this composer, with the best will in the world, a man himself of integrity amounting to saintliness, really conceived that this music was what would best serve the church.

[1] *Nicaea, A.M.* (1889) 160.

[2] Observe the melodies of *Gerontius, A.M.* 172, and *St. Drostane*, 99.

[3] Observe his predilection for an opening line of repeated notes in *St, Agnes,* 178, *Rievaulx,* 164, and *Ilkley, C.P.*291; the notable phrase which forms the second line of *Beatitudo,* 438 and the last of *Dominus Regit Me,* 197.

The secret of his style is, of course, the concert-goer's attitude which had infected the Victorian parish church. Hymns were made not to sing but for the people to listen to choirboys singing. And so the seductive melody and the part-song texture[1] come to the fore. In sum, then, we can describe Victorian church music as " tool-music " in the sense that it is composed with an eye to the " atmosphere " required by the church, and with an eye to the agreeable sensations which it would produce in the ears of the worshippers. It was composed in a self-conscious way which was unknown to the composers of the Puritan psalm-tunes or the music of the Wesleyan revival. Its degradation is due not to the fact that it is supposed to be serving the church but to the fact that in fact it is not serving the church at all but the arbitrary predilections of those who formed the influential membership of the parish churches of England. We shall deal in a moment with the reason for this statement.

One other aspect of religious " tool-music " is worth mentioning, and that is the growth of congregational singing amongst the prosperous nonconformists. With the slackening of Puritan disciplines in worship — the installation of organs, the segregation of the choir, the introduction of hymns and anthems as well as psalms—the heirs of the Reformation turned their attention to church music with a new interest. John Wesley had showed what could be done with song, and the Wesleyans of the nineteenth century incorporated into their worship a system of degenerate

[1] The worst example of his choral style is probably *Dies Irae, A.M.* 398.

church music which manifested in an exaggerated and even caricatured form the more evident qualities of eighteenth century English music ; the " fugal " tune paid homage to the *fugato* of eighteenth-century parlour-music, and the florid melody and poverty-stricken harmony of, for example, *Diadem*[1] to the part-songs of lighter eighteenth-century opera.

In Congregationalism, however, the development of congregational singing took a new turn with the establishment in 1848 of the Psalmody Class at Union Chapel, Islington,[2] directed by the minister (Dr. Henry Allon) and the organist (Dr. Henry John Gauntlett). To this class the whole congregation came weekly to learn the service music ; they sang hymns from the new hymnal which their minister and organist prepared,[3] and it was not long before they began to sing anthems as well. The idea of a semi-professional choir was still alien to the Puritan tradition of equality and democracy, but there was no longer thought to be any harm in the whole congregation performing a simple anthem, especially as anthems were, unlike hymns, strictly scriptural in their words. The result was the development in Congregationalism of hymn-tunes of strange complexity, resembling part-songs in being " interesting " enough to attract an amateur choral society, and, on the other hand, of anthems simple enough to be learnt by the same society on a few Monday evenings. In so far as this simplicity was a technical simplicity of broad melody

[1] *Methodist Hymn Book*, A.T. 6. The tune, often thought to be an " old " tune, was composed about 1840.

[2] Shortly followed by another similar class at Carr's Lane, Birmingham.

[3] *The Congregational Psalmist*, last edition, 1886.

and harmony, it was all to the good, and some of Gauntlett's best hymn-tunes show just this quality. But far more than this, "simplicity" meant to the congregation at Islington "what we are used to ", and was a quality not of the musical texture but of the musical idiom ; and so the door was flung wide open to the importation of much operatic idiom into sacred song.

Now this development is a very happy example of the effect on church-music of the energy, enterprise, and enthusiasm of the Victorian nonconformist (who was usually the fairly prosperous business-man). Once again, the emphasis is all on *action*—" Let us sing, never mind what we sing ". Action, not contemplation, use, not reverence, is the keynote of this as of other aspects of Victorian religion.

At this point, to sum up the degeneracy of music in the nineteenth century as a theological phenomenon, we would quote Augustine once again :

" It is the love of action that distracts the soul from the truth, and the origin of this love is pride. Pride is the vice which makes men prefer imitating God to serving Him. Rightly is it written in Scripture that ' the beginning of Pride is rebellion from God.' The soul swollen by pride goes forth beyond her own ' order ', becomes vain, and so (paradoxical though it appears) becomes less and less. . . . This is to place God far from her. . . ."

Superbia, or pride, is the word in which Augustine sums up the quality in man which precludes reverence, which manages and orders and thrusts itself into regions where management and ordering are not his province. Something of the kind had happened to Victorian England, and in thus identifying the root of bad music with the first of the cardinal sins, from which all other disorders spring, we bring ill-made music under a judgment more merciful and more inexorable than that of the purely musical critic.[1]

(*f*) MUSIC AS A HOME

We say that the judgment is merciful, and it must be so. For in thus representing bad music as the result of sin we have so far laid ourselves open to the charge of judging where we may not judge. What made people accept this music ? Whence comes the degeneration in the people's music from the traditional English folk-tune to the Victorian ditty ? If we can answer this question we shall see how the sin of which we have spoken was something in which the whole community was involved, and not by any means the sin of a few unscrupulous publishers and musicians.

Consider a few *obiter dicta* that have already appeared : we have mentioned the paradox, for example, that the Victorian church musician, though his music was so completely a product of corrupt thought and practice, was often himself a man of excellent and charitable ideals ; we have said that the people to whom the music we have mentioned appealed were those of the prosperous and possessing classes ; we have also hinted that what was thought to be " simple " music was really " music we are used to ". The end to which these hitherto unexplained comments

[1] The author asks leave to refer to four articles from his pen in the *Bulletin* of the Hymn Society (1948–9), dealing in detail with Wesley (Vol. II, No. 1), Dykes (II, 3, 5), Gauntlett (II, 5), and Sullivan (II, 7).

refer is this, that the badness of Victorian music is to be ascribed not only to the direct influence of the attitude of impatience and lack of reverence, but also to the homelessness and exile which overtook the people. "What we are used to"—still in most churches the normal criterion of good music—is identical with the symbol of security, and for the possessing classes no less than for the dispossessed, some symbol of security was urgently needed. It is the lack of tension, challenge, adventurousness, and judgment in Victorian music which makes it so flaccid, and it is precisely these qualities that made the worshipper cling to it so helplessly.

If we consider one more form of Victorian bad music we shall see this point much more clearly. I refer to the music of nineteenth century Revival. Now Revival in the nineteenth century, especially that which is associated in its later decades with the names of Dwight L. Moody and Ira D. Sankey, is the technique of ministering to the dispossessed and outcast on the collective principle. Mass-meetings and mass-salvation are the mainstays of the revivalist technique, and the revivals of the later nineteenth century brought the Gospel to many to whom the Bible was a closed book and the Church a barred mansion. One of the distinguishing marks of Revivalist technique is the emphasis in its preaching on judgment, together with the emphasis in its singing on peace. And singing played, on the whole, a greater part than preaching, certainly a greater part than reason, in the success of the movement.

Now Moody and Sankey came to England from America, where the technique of Revival had been

known for nearly a century, ever since the Kentucky
Revivals of 1797–1805. And they knew how much
the music of the Kentucky Revivals—the " negro
spirituals " had done for the success of the Gospel
there. They knew that under the stress of the
impact of the Gospel on the acute sufferings
and degradations of the American negroes a body
of music had been built up, the haunting
cadences and naive power of which half-hypnotised
everyone who heard it. Negro spiritual music is
born of the fire, and the quality of, say, *Were you there
when they crucified my Lord ?* is something which we
have not begun to analyse when we have ascribed it
to its use of the pentatonic scale. It is the quality
of burning and even suffering sincerity.

Moody and Sankey, then, in their revivals, sought
to make a similar use of folk-music, but when they
came to England the folk-music they found was not
what they perhaps had a right to expect. It should
have been *Greensleeves*, *Dives and Lazarus*, and the
rest of the contents of the *Oxford Book of Carols*.
But the dispossession of the ploughboy had meant the
dispossession of his music. For two centuries
Englishmen had hummed and whistled the ditties of
the continent, and now their folk-music was the
music-hall tune, which carried all the characteristics of
rhythmic and harmonic piquancy that were common
to the whole secular tradition of music at the time.
Therefore Ira D. Sankey, the musician of the team,
composed many tunes and adapted many others, all
in the style which should most easily appeal to their
listeners. The characteristic revivalist hymn-tune is
therefore jaunty in rhythm and rudimentary in

harmony, and this because that kind of music was "simple" for the people to whom the revivalist ministered. Simplicity for them was "what we are used to", the sophisticated, tawdry, often pretentious music which gave them some kind of escape from the drabness of their surroundings. The sixteenth-century farmer was at home with *Greensleeves* precisely because it was not an escape ; it was integrated with his work and his life, and on the whole he did not want to escape from that work and that life. That is why *Greensleeves* is in fact healthier and more hard-wearing than the hymns of Sankey. And we must say that the musical content of much of the Sankey-type hymnody is so low as to be infantile. The pretentious and succulent rhythm of Mrs. Knapp's *Behold Me Standing*, for example, is frankly nauseating to any musician of sensitiveness. The puerile technique of most of the work of Philipp Bliss (1838–76) arouses the wrath of the most tolerant critic. But consider the best, the least pretentious, and the most honourable and genuine of Sankey's own melodies—*There were Ninety and Nine*[1] ; it was composed, it is said, on the spur of the moment as a meeting was in progress. It is simple and although its harmony is impoverished, its rhythm is carol-like and its melody has a conspicuous climax. This we can regard as symbolic of a music designed for homeless people. It was what they were used to ; it proclaimed for them the gospel of peace "in the arms of Jesus". The fear-ridden populations of the industrial cities of England could not respond to challenge and austerity ; there was already too much of that in their lives. They

[1] *English Hymnal,* 584.

responded to a music which gave them the strongest feeling of exaltation with the minimum of effort. Its intellectual content might be tenuous to the point of illiteracy ; it might, and indeed did, correspond to the architecture of most modern cinemas and road-houses in its combination of the trivial and the pretentious. Its homeliness is an exaggerated and caricatured homeliness. But the working man and woman who find their heart's delight in this music are exactly in the position of the man who has spent thirty days on a raft in the Atlantic and is grateful for a warm bed and a sound house beyond which he need not set foot for a month. It is indeed everybody's business to give him back his " nerve " and send him to sea again in a seaworthy ship, for he cannot " come to himself " by remaining for ever in the house. But it is not the proper office of those people who have been spared the raft to grudge the man his hot water bottles or to call him a sinner or a coward for using them. Nor indeed may those who have been spared the raft themselves indulge in hot water bottles. No condemnation of hot water bottles and fires and warm blankets can be just which does not direct the greater part of its force on the earlier disaster which made them necessary.

This astonishing outbreak of illiterate and poverty-stricken music has therefore to be seen as the product, at several removes, of the same force which produced the bad music of the cathedral and the parish church. It is, once again, *amor agendi*—the love of " results ".

Why then did all this happen in a religious context ? To that question we can only answer by quoting the old proverb : *corruptio optimi pessima*. It is in that

religious context that man's conscience is raw, that
his experience is most elemental, that the judgment of
the Word beats upon him. If he meets that judgment
with penitence the result is the making of a " new
creature " ; if he reacts against it with pride, self-
justification, and fear, the result is the reverse of
creative ; it is corrupting. Therefore it is in the
religious context that the deepest corruptions, the
most terrifying cruelties, the most pernicious lies are
brought to being. Our next chapter will tell something of a turn in the tide ; but whether we blame or
whether we praise any age of church music, no
category other than the theological will give us sound
ground for judging.

(f) CHURCH MUSIC ON THE CONTINENT

To the general thesis that music in the nineteenth
century church suffered a notable decline in taste
the music of the Lutheran and Roman Catholic
countries gives no ground for objection. But the
reasons for this decline were somewhat differently
assorted from those which we have associated with
English church music. The most important way
in which Continental church music differs from that
of England in its development is in the fact that both
the Lutheran and the Roman Catholic churches,
from the time respectively of the Reformation and the
Counter-Reformation, had an immense treasury of
great music upon which succeeding generations were
content to draw. The Lutheran church, being more
modest in its demands, was content with the smaller
store, but the heritage of sixteenth-century chorales

which still forms, with a few unimportant exceptions, the repertory of the present-day Lutheran congregation, was a perfect instrument for its purposes. On the same principle, the Golden Age of polyphony produced, in the works of Palestrina, Lassus, Byrd, Victoria, and their followers a body of church music which is sufficient for all the normal requirements of the largest and best-appointed Catholic cathedral. Preoccupied as the continental musicians were from 1700 onwards with the new classical music, they tended to give of their second best to the church ; and in those countries where the classical idiom found its highest expressions the decadence of church music is in general most marked.

It would have been well enough, of course, had this decadence taken the form simply of a failure to compose new music and a reliance on the treasuries of the sixteenth century ; but this was far from being the case. The operatic style did in fact affect Roman Catholic music seriously, and the infiltration of decadent Roman Catholic music into Lutheran and Anglican circles had an unfortunate effect on their already tarnished repertoire. Since the removal in 1829 of the Disabilities of English Catholics, and the subsequent re-establishment of the Roman hierarchy in this country, Roman Catholic hymnody has contributed more meretricious melody and sickly harmony to the *corpus* of Victorian hymnody than many Protestant singers realise ; and the same is true in a less degree of the Lutheran church, which has allowed a certain amount of Catholic melody to flow into its treasury of Lutheran chorales. The most obvious example, to take only one, is the ubiquity of

the hymn-tune which is known as *Hursley*[1] and associated in many hymn-books with Keble's *Sun of my
soul*. This melody is found in two or three different
forms in English hymn-books and also in several
contemporary Lutheran choral-books. It is of Roman
Catholic origin and its highly sentimental melody and
harmony derive directly from the more maudlin
forms of Italian opera. The contents of the first
edition of the *Westminster Hymnal* and of Hemy's
Easy Music for Church Choirs (1852) are of an almost
uniformly debased standard.

But in as much as the countries of Europe were
affected less violently than our own by the first impact
of the Industrial Revolution, a certain amount of folk-
music has always had its place in the music of continental Christendom, and its influence has been healthy,
if less distinctive in the Latin countries than in those
of the north. And it is by no means fanciful to
point out that music which appears to the English
mind astonishingly sentimental and demonstrative is
less outrageous to the mind of, say, an Italian Catholic
than to that of a middle-class Englishman simply
because the cultural and social backgrounds of the
countries are widely different.

One thing is certain, however, namely that the
Roman Catholic church never lost its hold on its
metaphysical or dogmatic obligations as the Protestant
church did in the nineteenth century. The tradition
that the Vatican should have something to say about
music in the church did not by any means die with the
Counter-Reformation. A whole series of papal documents bears witness to the concern which the Popes

[1] *A.M.* 24.

genuinely felt for the preservation of good and healthy music in the church. With these we may not deal here, but we must mention briefly the circumstances which led up to the publication of the celebrated *Motu Proprio* of Pius X in 1903.

Conscious of the relapse of taste which had over-taken Roman Catholic church music, certain Christian musicians set their hands to a revival of the pure polyphony of Palestrina and the austerity of Gregorian melody. In Germany especially this new *a cappella* style flourished, especially in the hands of Eduard Grell (1800–86) and Heinrich Bellermann (1852–1903). New collections of ancient music, variously edited, appeared in the libraries, and a spirit character-ised by Paul Henry Lang[1] as " pious antiquarianism " pervaded the Roman Catholic church of the Continent. Prominent in this work were the various " Cecilian Societies ", which originated in an English musical society in 1785 but soon spread to the continent and to America. But there was never more than a derivative quality about the music that was produced under these auspices, and, what was far worse, the editions of Palestrina and his school that these enthusiasts pro-duced were models of what such editions should not be. The confusion thus created in continental musical taste can be read of in any textbook[2]; what is im-portant here is that it was the occasion for the great reforms inspired by Popes Leo XIII and Pius X. The incursion of sophisticated organ-playing into the Roman rites caused Pope Leo XIII to issue in 1886

[1] Op. cit., p. 854.
[2] Lang, op. cit., p. 1008.

a decree restricting the use of the organ in church-music. Four years before a congress at Arezzo for the improvement of church-music issued in the foundation of an international Society to continue this work. The Benedictines of Solesmes began the publication in 1889 of their *Paleographia Musicale* which has become normative for all modern editions of Gregorian plainchant ; and in 1903, as the climax of this series of reforms, Pope Pius X issued a *Motu Proprio*[1] in which very careful instructions are given for the guidance of church musicians all over the Catholic world.

Compared with the edict of John XXII the *Motu Proprio* is a longer, more detailed, and more carefully composed document. It consists of nine chapters dealing respectively with General Principles, the different kinds of sacred music, the inviolability of the Liturgical Text, the limitations of the eternal form of sacred compositions, the conduct and training required of church musicians, the use of instruments in church, the vital necessity that music be subordinate to the liturgy, the establishment of *Scholae Cantorum*, and, in conclusion, the necessity of carrying these reforms into effect. A few quotations will bring out the important points in this document. In the following we hear a distinct echo from 1325 and from the Fathers :

" Sacred music should . . . possess in the highest degree the qualities proper to the liturgy, and precisely sanctity and goodness of form, from which

---

[1] The document in translation can be obtained from the Publisher to the Holy See, Burns, Oates, and Washbourne, under the title *Catholic Church Music* (1933). Our quotations are taken from that edition.

its other character of universality spontaneously springs. It must be holy, and therefore, exclude all profanity not only in itself but in the manner in which it is presented." (Par. 2.)

The Gregorian chant is held up as the model for all sacred music :

" The more closely a composition for church approaches in its movement, inspiration, and savour the Gregorian form, the more sacred and liturgical it becomes." (Par. 3.)

A reflection on current nineteenth-century usage of the kind to which we have attended in this chapter appears a little later :

" Among the different kinds of modern music that which appears less suitable for accompanying the functions of public worship is the theatrical style, which was in the greatest vogue, especially in Italy, during the last century. This of its very nature is diametrically opposed to the Gregorian Chant and the classic polyphony, and therefore to the most important law of all good music. Besides the intrinsic structure, the rhythm and what is known as the conventionalism of this style adapt themselves but badly to the requirements of true liturgical music." (Par. 6.)

Here once again do we hear the voice of the Fathers speaking in the modern idiom :

" The employment of the piano is forbidden in church, as is also that of noisy and frivolous instruments such as drums, cymbals, bells and the like." (Par. 19.)

And again

> " It is not permitted to have the chant preceded by
> long preludes or to interrupt it with intermezzo
> pieces. The sound of the organ as an accompani-
> ment to the chant . . . must be governed not only
> by the special nature of the instrument but must
> participate in all the qualities proper to sacred
> music as above described." (Pars. 17-18.)

The instructions concerning the settings of the Mass
include the demand that the *Kyrie*, *Gloria*, *Credo*,
etc., of the Mass shall be composed as continuous
pieces and not as series of pieces forming complete
compositions in themselves ; that is, the *Mass in D*
of Beethoven (in this particular respect) would conform
with these instructions, but the *Mass in B minor* of
Bach, in which the *Credo* (for example) consists of a
large number of separate musical numbers, would
not (par. 11). Women's voices are solemnly prohibited in church, and it is also commanded that the
singers of the choir should be as far as possible hidden
from the view of the congregation (pars 13 and 14).
The organ is forbidden to accompany the Gregorian
chant of the Celebrant, and solo-singing in the choir
is to be strictly regulated in such a way that it contains
no trace and gives no opportunity for the unsuitable
projection of the individual personality (par. 12).

These reforms have had only sporadic success ;
but in as much as the internal discipline of the Church
of Rome is at present at a far higher level than it was
in the fourteenth century, the respect paid to papal
decrees in the Roman Catholic world is greater.
Moreover continental Catholics were glad enough to be

recalled from the extravagances of Bruckner and Liszt with which they became quickly sated. Perhaps the improvement of Roman Catholic taste in church music is to be seen at its most impressive in the music of the Cathedral of Westminster, where the work of the late Richard Runciman Terry (1865–1938) has had such good success. But the process of reviving the taste of so far-flung a community as the Roman Catholic church, which suffered not a little from the diseases we have noticed as afflicting Protestant church music in England, is necessarily a slow process, and the indications at present, nearly fifty years after the promulgation of the *Motu Proprio*, are certainly more encouraging than those which we inferred from the comments of John Wyclif[1] fifty years after the edict of John XXII.

[1] See page 105.

CHAPTER IX

THE TWENTIETH CENTURY

The Religious temper of the Century—Twentieth Century
Theology—Extra-Christian Civilisation—Music in the
Twentieth Century—Music in the Twentieth-century
Church.

(a) THE RELIGIOUS TEMPER OF THE CENTURY

In its religious temper our own century is very
clearly connected by development and reaction with
the preceding. We have said that the preoccupation
of the nineteenth-century European family was
security. The developments of this in the present
age take at least three forms.

First, this preoccupation with security, born of the
elemental fear of homelessness, has proceeded from the
domestic and individual to the international level.
States are now where families were a hundred years ago
—desperately and irrationally afraid of dispossession ;
the prosperous nations fear the claims of the less
prosperous and the smaller nations are already under-
going the grievous process of " absorption " in large
nations.

Secondly, the fear of insecurity at the domestic
level has issued in a strong reaction which has taken
the form of state-organised social services, increasing
state control of industrial enterprise, the more or less
violent reclamation by the poor of the possessions of
the prosperous, and an increase of that legalised neigh-
bourliness which is the best aspect of socialism.

But, thirdly, the fear of insecurity has been replaced in the public mind by something less elemental and less healthy, namely a sense of grievance between classes. The issue has developed from the battle by a class for its rights into a battle between classes each claiming the other's rights. The identification of the church with the prosperous classes of the nineteenth century, especially in Protestant countries, has led to a sense of grievance against the church in whole sections of the population, and this, coupled with the increased responsibility which the State has undertaken for the welfare of the citizens, has completed the process of secularisation which, but for the Reformers, might well have been completed three centuries before.

It is therefore the outstanding characteristic of the religious temper of our century that for the first time since the days of Constantine it is possible for a man to live a complete life (humanly speaking) without any kind of reference to the Christian church. Religious qualifications for any kind of social or economic or political position no longer exist. For what the Industrial Revolution did for the Protestant countries the continental revolutions in politics have done for the Catholic countries. The Church, in fact, is now completely divorced in the public mind from public affairs. It has become a " separate " institution ; membership of it is in a new way a matter of conscious choice in most countries, and in the remaining countries it has become a matter of actual personal danger, for as the reader is well aware the new age of political persecution is now fully come.

(*b*) TWENTIETH CENTURY THEOLOGY

The church's answer to this situation has been manifold. We cannot here go into the matter of internal church-organisation ; we can only refer to the effect on the contemporary church of the economic disfranchisement of a very large proportion of its officers ; and we have already referred to the closing of ranks which has been apparent both in the revival of " Catholic Action " among the Roman Catholics and the ecumenical movements in the Protestant churches. These are natural developments for which there is plenty of evidence and which need no further comment. But it is worth noting that in theology a development has taken place which, when future historians of doctrine set themselves to disentangle it, may be found to have its focal point in the concept of *Reason*.

Now Reason as a non-religious faculty made a dramatic appearance (by no means its first) at the Enlightenment in the eighteenth century. Reason, then, employed by theologians and critics, produced on the one hand plain scepticism of Christian dogma and on the other a " liberal " critical attitude which was responsible for the great growth of Biblical and historical scholarship that marks the later decades of the nineteenth century.[1] The importance of this work must not be underestimated by those who see clearly, and properly, the excesses to which it was taken by the irresponsible. A tendency to read the

[1] The growth of linguistic study bore characteristic fruit in the production of the Revised Version of the Bible in 1881-95, and in the Westcott and Hort edition of the Greek New Testament, followed in 1910 by Alexander Souter's standard Oxford Text.

Bible as if it could be judged entirely by the standards applicable to a directory or a text-book became part of the tradition of Liberal Protestantism, and a strong reaction against the supernatural led to a considerable degree of perversity in many quarters.[1]

Againt this the so-called " theology of crisis " was launched in Germany and Switzerland during the First World War by the teaching of Karl Barth and his followers, who owed much, but not all, of their inspiration to Sören Kierkegaard, and who preached a gospel of Judgment such as had not been heard in Protestant circles since the seventeenth century.[3] It was not unnatural that the emphasis in this way of thought was placed entirely on the theological concept of Grace, and that the scope of Reason was severely limited. Reason, it says, falls under the judgment of original sin and needs redemption. In this way the excesses of rationalism were combated from the Continent.

But there is a new force in the word " reason " which has now to be reckoned with, namely the results, fragmentary and dubiously estimable though they are, of universal education, the growth of the Press and broadcasting. A newly educated public has called for, and formed the material for, a new age of Christian apologetic. In Catholic circles the orthodox humanism and rational dogmatism of such as Jacques

[1] Criticism carried to greater lengths gave rise to the " New Theology ", whose spearhead was Dr. R. J. Campbell's book of that name, published in 1900. A generation earlier, however, the critical attitude had been anticipated by Bishop Colenso's *The Pentateuch and the Book of Joshua Critically Examined* (1862).

[3] For a good summary of this theological attitude see H. R. Mackintosh, *Types of Modern Theology* (1937), Chh. VII-VIII.

Maritain, together with a notable revival of the theology of St. Thomas Aquinas by the Dominicans, has made a great impression, and in Protestant circles in our own country the way has been led by such distinguished lay people as Mr. C. S. Lewis and Miss Dorothy Sayers both of whom have succeeded in writing best-sellers which deal with the plain doctrines of the Christian Faith.[1] The preaching of our churches has admitted afresh the ancient and honourable practice of exposition, enriched by the new scholarship. Scholarship itself, through the work of such men as Dr. C. H. Dodd, has admitted that reason and reverence are not enemies but brothers. The conclusion of the issue between Science and Religion is no longer, as it once was, foregone in favour of the scientist. A new technique of " revival " has therefore appeared in our time, namely the Revival through reason which is shown in such diverse ways as the Missions to the Universities (in which the late Archbishop William Temple took a leading part), the Christian Commando Campaigns (organised in the first instance during the Second World War by the Methodist Connexion), the Roman Catholic " Sword of the Spirit ", and the revival of the Iona Community under Dr. George MacLeod. Samuel Johnson's liberal, imaginative, and evangelical hymn " City of God "[2] does for the intellectuals of the present day what ' The ninety and nine " did for the dispossessed of the nineteenth century.

[1] C. S. Lewis, *The Problem of Pain* (1940), *Broadcast Talks* (1941), *Christian Behaviour* (1943), *Beyond Personality* (1945), *The Screwtape Letters* (1942). Dorothy Sayers, *The Mind of the Maker* (1941) and *The Man Born to be King* (1942).

[2] *Songs of Praise* (1931), 468.

But the hold of the church on those people whom Moody and Sankey evangelised has for the moment weakened. Entertainment and information are now universal, and the church finds itself a struggling competitor in fields, where for a millennium and a half it has held the monopoly.

The metaphysical struggle then is centred at present on the issue between the rational and the irrational. The Church has on the one hand seen clearly the results of perverted science and scholarship ; on the other it has seen the results of romantic superstition and idolatry. Secular society, which is now virtually extra-Christian society, has received the benefits of education and has yet learned to use the words "academic", "highbrow", and "cultured", as words of reproach. This conflict, which is really the process of sorting out the Word or Logos of the ancient apologists from the human applications and perversions of the *faculty* of Logos (which again Justin the Apologist was prepared to distinguish from the Divine Word) has an important bearing on what we shall have to say about music.

(c) EXTRA-CHRISTIAN CIVILISATION

If the Church has thus faced the issue of Reason, it has been alone in facing it fairly. For a characteristic of the twentieth century which is far less ambiguously apparent is the increase on all sides in extra-Christian society of " relativism ", or the tendency to construct systems of thinking that abandon the notion of central or supernatural authority altogether. Totalitarian politics place all their faith in the crudest forms of autocratic and irresponsible human authority, and in so doing proclaim themselves idolatries. But at the other extreme the abandonment of accepted, even unwritten, moral standards at the domestic level and the philosophies (such as Logical Positivism) which base themselves on the absence of supernatural Truth are the outcome of the identification by the nation at large of the Church with the iniquity of the irresponsible rulers in society and industry. The State has never shown itself a trustworthy vessel for the preservation of the supernatural standards and doctrines ; the rejection of the Church has therefore meant the rejection also of the doctrines. The resulting confusion in society, from the abiding threat of international war to the collapse of common morals in the family and the home, is a natural development of the rejection of metaphysical authority, and those who erect these instinctive reactions into philosophical systems that justify the instincts can be properly and technically described by men of Christian presuppositions as idolators.

(d) MUSIC IN THE TWENTIETH CENTURY

Now music in the twentieth century has faithfully reflected all these tendencies. The dramatic suddenness with which the " European orthodoxy " of the Bach-Brahms school was dropped by musicians is a historical curiosity which is beyond our power fully to explain. Brahms died in 1897, and the turn of the century witnessed in all European music two unmistakable tendencies, namely the return to musical nationalism in the revival in all countries of distinctive styles based on folk-music, and the swift evolution of experimental techniques. The music of Jan Sibelius

(b. 1865) in Finland, of Bela Bartok (1881–1945)
and Zoltan Kodaly (b. 1882) in Hungary, of Enrique
Granados (1867–1916) and Manuel de Falla (1876–
1948) in Spain, and in our own country of Ralph
Vaughan Williams (b. 1872) shows the new nationalism ; while the "impressionistic" techniques of
Claude Debussy (1862–1918), Maurice Ravel (1875–
1937), Francois Poulenc (b. 1899) and the school of
Nadia Boulanger in France, and the revolutionary
aesthetic and technique of the atonalists of Vienna,
Arnold Schönberg (b. 1874) and Alban Berg (1885–
1935) excellently exemplify the new experimentalism.

It will be observed that in those countries where
" European orthodoxy " received the least hospitality
the national music gains the surest foothold.   This is
obviously true of Hungary, Spain, England, and in a
slightly different way of France.   All of these,
especially England, had a lively national idiom which
was completely overlaid in the ninetheenth century by
the European idiom, and therefore no composers of
the front rank appeared from them during that time.
On the other hand, Vienna, the natural home of
" European orthodoxy ", has produced the most
violent of the new experiments, and has given the
modern world its best music in the non-tonal work of
Berg,   notably   the   opera   *Wozzeck*.   Prussian
Germany, the birthplace of Bach and Brahms,
has contributed relatively little to modern music
beyond the work of Richard Strauss (1864–1949)
which remains firmly settled in the idiom of the
nineteenth century, with suggestive embellishments
from the repertory of Wagner.   Russia, as might
be expected,   after   a   brief   incursion,   in   the

works of Glinka (1803–57), Tchaikovsky (1840–93) and Rachmaninoff (1873–1943) and some spectacularly experimental work in Scriabin (1872–1915) and the earlier Stravinsky (b. 1882) has now firmly established itself in a folk-idiom ; this is arbitrarily controlled from the political headquarters of the Soviet State, and therefore stands in greater danger of artificiality and the character technically described in that country as " bourgeois " than did any of the earlier music which is now roundly condemned in Moscow.

(*e*) MUSIC IN THE TWENTIETH CENTURY CHURCH

Now in church music during this century we observe two characteristics which are not unexpected ; namely, that on the one hand the music of the church embraces the new nationalism with considerable alacrity and the new artificial experiments not at all, and on the other it preserves a greater proportion than secular music of the legacy of the nineteenth century. This is the same as saying that in the church continuity is preserved in a greater degree than outside it. The tendency of the church to be nervous of human inventions—even when it has turned out that the hesitation was purely precautionary—has already been mentioned, and is well known, especially to its detractors. This hesitation has, of course, been the result of the necessity under which any responsible organ of the Church must refer any new invention to categories of judgment far more profound and numerous than those with which the non-religious thinker has to deal. Atonal church music, therefore, is hardly to be found at all. But that music which preserves the tradition of the immediate past, and that which preserves the tradition of the remote past, are both to be found in twentieth century church music, because this is the invariable policy of the church in such matters.

We shall deal here briefly with the tendencies to be observed in English church music for the same reason that we applied to our study of the nineteenth century ; it is in England, as it happens, that all the tendencies are to be seen most sharply defined.

The continuation of the nineteenth century tradition has resulted in a considerable output of church music of a standard far higher than the " decadent " secular music of the same period. Correspondingly the best work of the musicians of the nineteenth century " renaissance ", especially Hubert Parry (1848–1918), and Charles Villiers Stanford (1852–1924) was certainly their music for religious occasions. In Parry and Stanford[1] we see a very healthy attempt to produce a church music which would not stray beyond the confines of nineteenth century tonal and harmonic traditions, but which should for all that be original, sound, and without sentimentality. Parry maintains a high standard of craftsmanship and integrity throughout his choral works, and even when these are not liturgical pieces, they are almost always strongly Christian, not to say ecclesiastical, in idiom and context. His *Blest Pair of Sirens*, is, of course, an acknowledged classic of English choral music, and his *Songs of Farewell* are perhaps the greatest, as they are almost the last, of his many devotional pieces. This music stands somewhere between the great

[1] See J. A. Fuller Maitland, *The Music of Parry and Stanford* (1934).

classical Masses and liturgical church music ; it is not strictly ecclesiastical but equally certainly it is not secular. For our purposes it can certainly be regarded as " church music ".

Stanford, a bolder and more variable composer than Parry, put some of his best work into purely liturgical music, bringing to perfection an almost symphonic style of service-writing in his great Services in B flat, C, F, and G ; his purpose was to introduce a sense of musical form as well as a reverent and careful setting of the words of the Anglican service, and the musical result is highly satisfying. In his *Stabat Mater* (1907) he draws more freely than any English composer ever dared upon the style of the Italian opera, taking Verdi's *Requiem* as his model ; this work is the zenith of the English " theatrical " style in church music, being perhaps the only work of its period which combines remarkable stylistic *abandon* with the honesty which was denied to the composers whose work we criticised in the last chapter.

Edward Elgar is known as the greatest English musician since Purcell, and although his output is as a matter of fact extremely unequal, his greatest work amply justifies this judgment. His church music, of which there is not a great deal, is clearly " occasional " music and its idiom is unmistakably under the influence of Catholic nineteenth century church music ; it is therefore highly sentimental and by no means characteristic of the composer of the *E flat Symphony*, the *Introduction and Allegro for Strings*, and *The Dream of Gerontius*.[1]

---

[1] We remind the reader that we do not regard Oratorio as " church music " in the strict sense. See chapter VII.

The traditional path has been followed by many composers of the following generation. A great quantity of tedious and unprofitable music must be admitted ; and we have to record with regret the continuance of a pseudo-Sankey style in a good deal of the music that is still produced for the use of young people in nonconformist circles. But perhaps the finest music in the older idiom which we have in the English church is that of Edward Bairstow (1874–1946), who has brought it to heights which it will almost certainly never reach again ; his work is entirely for the Cathedral choir and for solo organ, and the standard it maintains through its not very considerable compass is of the highest.

The vital development of a national idiom in England, however, has been received by the English Church with great pride and welcome. Perhaps this revival of English music through the folk-song may be dated from the publication of *The English Hymnal* in 1906. For a good account of the character and fate of this book the reader is referred to Louis F. Benson's book, *The English Hymn*. All we wish to notice here is that in this book for the first time the nineteenth century idiom was not taken for granted as the normal idiom for English hymnody. The folk-music of England was harnessed to the words of familiar hymns, and the great chorales and psalm-tunes of the Reformation, which nineteenth century orthodoxy had disguised under key-signatures and bar-lines were restored to their ancient tonality and rhythm. Plainsong was revived and the Victorian hymnody was severely restricted. The fact that this book has survived to be a best-seller in Anglican circles to-day whereas the less radically reforming *Hymns Ancient and Modern* of 1904 was a failure from the start and has long been out of print, is an historical curiosity into which we may not enter here. It was the *English Hymnal* which, along with a good deal of liberal Anglo-Catholic theological atmosphere, introduced the English church to native English music ; and its editor was Ralph Vaughan Williams.

The significance of Vaughan Williams in this story is pivotal. In the English Hymnal we have, of course, the only example in English hymnody, and the only example at all since Goudimel's edition of the Genevan Psalters in 1543, of a hymn-book edited by a musician who subsequently achieved international respect. Vaughan Williams is not now primarily regarded as a church-musician, but his influence on church-music has been vital. He has developed in his composition a style which goes back to the roots of English music, not only folk-music but also the ecclesiastical *organum* of the tenth century. (The reincarnation of *organum* in his use of parallel fifths is referred to by any critic who comments on his music). As his music has developed, the folk-idiom and the idiom of the early church has become more and more an integral part of its texture ; and correspondingly the music has carried more and more authority, until the thunderclap of the Sixth Symphony burst over England in 1948 ; and the reception which the musical public has given to this symphony indicates the mastery with which the composer has forged his tools, handled his material, and conveyed his message.

Many composers have followed more or less closely in this way, and the *corpus* of English church music is growing in quantity and in quality. A notable rise in the musical taste of all denominations of the English church has taken place ; music of all standards of difficulty and profundity but of a strangely high standard of integrity continued to appear. At the risk of invidiousness we refer to two examples— Armstrong Gibbs, *I the Prisoner of the Lord* and William Harris's *Be Strong in the Lord*—as examples of modern English church music which employ an idiom which is neither derived from the nineteenth century nor affectedly " folky " or, as it were, " pre-Raphaelite ".

Although this improvement in musical taste has made its first appearance in the Church of England, ecumenical tendencies coupled with the enormous increase in the opportunities of hearing and judging music of all kinds have made Christians more ready to learn from one another in musical matters. So we find that the nonconformist denominations have, with varying success and dexterity, taken leaves from the *English Hymnal* for new editions of their own hymn-books ; and correspondingly we find a new growth of congregational singing, once the monopoly of the Free Churches, in the parish churches and cathedrals of our country.

Less immediately apparent but not less certain is the new attitude which the church is adopting towards the musician. Formerly the church's answer to the autonomy which the musician has claimed with increasing firmness ever since 1600 was on the one hand to limit, either by decree or by the force of public opinion, the range of music that could qualify for the description " religious ", and on the other to encourage, by the same force of public opinion, the notion that the artist, having claimed this autonomy, was something of an outcast and a prodigal. In the present age, however, the church, which is itself far less than formerly entangled with social prejudices and conventions, is finding itself able to approach musicians who are not to be regarded as primarily church musicians, and by commissioning works from them to acknowledge that in the spiritual autonomy they have claimed there is not only rebellion but also, and primarily, a core of justice and truth. The Three Choirs' Festivals in the West Country are, in our own country, the most familiar occasions on which music, both classical and commissioned, is sung and played as an act of worship ; and the adventure of St. Matthew's, Northampton, in commissioning a series of liturgical works from musicians of the front rank is a bold development of the same policy. The church, in fact, is being brought to recognise that the musician has an offering of his own to bring, that he has a language of his own to speak, and that neither may the offering be judged nor the language checked by propositions in dogmatics and ecclesiastical discipline.

To this we have nothing new to add from the evidence supplied by the continental churches. The *Motu Proprio* of Pius X has influenced Roman Catholic taste in varying measure ; so far as a revival has occurred, however, it has been more a revival of medieval plainsong than a re-baptism of native folk-idioms. The Confessional Church of Germany, it may be remarked, saw a notable revival of chorale-writing during the Nazi persecutions between 1933 and 1945, and some fine tunes in modal idioms were

213

the result. But it is not unfair to say that the increasing disorganisation of continental politics, social and ecclesiastical, has greatly hindered a free and healthy development of church music.

CHAPTER X

TOWARDS A CHRISTIAN JUDGMENT

In the foregoing pages Christian judgment and
Christian uses of music have presented themselves in
various forms. It now remains for us to make some
attempt to answer the question, what are the scope
and limits of Christian judgment on music? But
before we do that, we must note that the context
within which all Christian judgments are made has
undergone a violent change in the decades since the
Second World War.

At the present time (1966) we have been forced
down to a redefinition of the boundary between the
sacred and the secular. At the time when I wrote
the foregoing pages (1945) it was still possible to be
tolerably certain what one was talking about when one
talked of " sacred music "—or sacred anything. That
is to say, one could talk dogmatically on such matters
without ignoring a too impressive body of opinion.
To dogmatize now is possible only by ignoring a very
large, conspicuous and vocal body of opinion.

Not to stray beyond the limits which this essay
originally set itself, we may attend to the very significant and controversial gestures that have been made
in church music since the publication of Geoffrey
Beaumont's *Folk Mass* in 1956.[1] What we want to
ask here is—what would the primitive Christians have
thought about this? Beaumont pleaded in his
apologia for the use of very popular and naive music

[1] Published by Josef Weinberger, London.

215

in Christian worship that this was exactly the kind of thing which the early Christians did. But the conclusion to which the documents inevitably lead is quite the reverse. True—the primitive Christians, when they began to make judgments, made them (as we have said) in a manner which modern thought about music has called into question. They tended to follow a Platonic line in proscribing certain instruments and styles. But they did proscribe them ; and if they tended to say that music associated with the theatre was unsuitable for use in Christian worship, then they must necessarily have said that music reminiscent of the pantomime (which Beaumont's is, by design) is on the far side of the secular boundary. Beaumont's original argument will not stand up for a moment.

But this hardly helps us towards a Christian judgment, because we have been suggesting that naive judgments of the kind recorded in our earlier documents will not serve us nowadays. So far as our question goes, we are no further on if we say that John Chrysostom would not have cared for Beaumont. He would not have cared for many Christian post-war judgments about sex or about money.

The second half of the twentieth century is witnessing a good deal more than the Beaumont gesture. We have (as I have said in *Twentieth Century Church Music*, whose details I do not want to repeat here) electronic music, twelve-tone music, music which employs every kind of sophistication developed in the secular field, all offered to the church. Church music-making, in these days of rapid communication, is now a lively conversation, at times becoming a dispute, between people who are asking different questions, making

different protests, and producing very widely different
kinds of music.

For example : take the particular matter of the
public performance of the psalms. The situation in
the Anglican churches of the year, say, 1939 was a
straight choice between singing them to plainsong and
singing them to Anglican chants. (I limit this to
Anglican churches because it is there that the psalms
are more habitually and fully employed in worship
than in any other branch of the Church.) Certain
questions were hardly beginning to be asked by
church musicians—such as whether the psalms should
be sung at all, and whether those were the only two
choices open if one did sing them.

The Catholic liberal revival produced a new gesture
in the early fifties—the psalmody of Joseph Gélineau,[1]
which by now has become well known in many
branches of the Church. Originally a singing device
of French origin, it has been the subject of much
experiment in English churches, and especially in
non-Anglican churches. For a time there was great
enthusiasm for this technique. It was still at its
height when I wrote (1961–2) *Twentieth Century
Church Music.* It was a liberation in three ways—in
being congregationally practicable without carrying
the archaistic associations of plainsong : in introducing
a new kind of music which was recognizably modern
yet essentially traditional : and in introducing a technique of singing which, though medieval in origin, was
unfamiliar to most of those who became enthusiastic
about it, namely the antiphonal style of " verse " and
" chorus ".

[1] Published by The Grail, London.

But now the conversation has gone further. People have said that Gélineau has not had the last word. Continuing to write in an antiphonal style, composers such as Christopher Dearnley,[1] Arthur Wills[2] and Peter Tranchell[3] have been writing new music for the psalms which all three would especially claim is " English " in a sense in which Gélineau is rather emphatically " French ". Moreover, the last two of these composers have intentionally adopted styles which owe everything to secular music—the bumpy, exuberant popular style of Wills, and the rich and colourful operatic style of Tranchell.

Gélineau, one feels, would have pleased the primitive Church, while Wills and Tranchell would not. But I mention this process only as an illustration of the conversation and controversy that is at present so lively in church music.

Another gesture which is worth recording is that of the composer who has a continuing belief in the twelve-tone style of music, but sets himself to make it intelligible for church use. Frederick Rimmer's " Sing we Merrily " is an example.[4] This piece impresses any careful listener primarily as a very simple and colourful setting of part of Psalm 81. The fact that it is a fairly consistent twelve-tone piece in the style of Schoenberg in no way obtrudes itself on the listener. It is a casual point so far as he is concerned. The composer, in that piece, regarded it as a challenge worth taking up, to write a piece in a contemporary

[1] Published in the Salisbury Diocesan Festival Music Book for 1965.
[2] To be published by Novello.
[3] Unpublished at present (1966) but performed in Cambridge.
[4] Published 1963 by Novello.

style which would be liturgically useful precisely because it obtruded its modernity at no point : it is tolerably easy to sing, and appropriate as a setting of its words. It *sounds* like ecstatic prophecy, which is what Psalm 81 is about.

Yet there are many musicians writing to-day whose styles are by no means contemporary. The best of them write their own music, not second-hand music : but the influences which they show are ancient rather than modern. Their music can have, as the music of Herbert Howells for example has, perfect integrity without attempting to assimilate non-tonal or popular styles.

One must also bring in evidence the fact that more than ever nowadays composers of international secular renown are writing for the Church : Britten, Berkeley, Walton in England : Samuel Barber in the United States : Frank Martin in Switzerland : and of course the incomparable Stravinsky. Where the church is operating on a large and ecumenical scale, the market for music of the most exalted kind is wider than it ever was. Britten's *War Requiem* became a " best seller " from the moment of its first performance in 1962. Foundations like Coventry Cathedral, or modern universities, or large choral societies, which are often fairly well removed from the traditional parochial life of the Church, are inviting the best composers to give of their best. The story is quite different (though not wholly discreditable) at parish level. The duty of the parish church musician to-day is a matter of very free and widespread discussion, and it is possible that the modern folk-singer may turn out to be one of his useful, if still neglected, guides.

However—all at present is debate and discussion. What, in this context, is Christian judgment ?

It can, I believe, be carried out in two planes. The confusion of tongues that besets us at present is no reason for the Church's abandoning a detached and philosophical approach to contemporary problems. It can make theological judgments still, and it should. Therefore I stand wholly by the account of this which I gave in the first edition of this book, and which I now present again to the reader.

Judgment based on Traditional Theology

We begin from the assumption, for which there is sound ground in Christian and pre-Christian thought, that the metaphysical and physical worlds are kingdoms with a common frontier. Plato's theory of the communication between the world of " forms " and the phenomenal world is an early and celebrated statement of this truth. Christian teaching, characteristically rich and varied in its imagery, expresses the same truth when it says that God took flesh, that God works in history, that spiritual realities may be laid hold on through such material things as bread, wine, and water (this we call the doctrine of sacraments), and that " the Kingdom of heaven is within you ". The Christian doctrine of the Incarnation is that the Word became Flesh, which is to say, among other things, that the metaphysical became physical, that truth was translated into act, that there is communication, and in certain conditions community, between the Ideal (pictured in Scripture as " heaven ") and the Actual (pictured as " earth ").

Consider, then, the metaphysical and the physical under a political analogy as two kingdoms sharing a long frontier. The truth about art will be sufficiently stated under the same figure if we say that it is a subordinate kingdom or " county " autonomous in some but not in all things, lying *across* that frontier, part of it in the metaphysical and part of it in the physical kingdom ; very much as the county of Sussex lies partly in the western and partly in the eastern hemispheres. We may further think of this " county " as having three seats of legislation, one in the metaphysical and one in the physical half to administer local bye-laws, and one on the frontier which administers the whole county and which is known as " aesthetic ". From the subordinate county-towns proceed the laws of grammar and technique on the metaphysical side and those of moral and practical application (including " performance ") on the other ; these bye-laws are diversified, of course, through the various " lateral " divisions of the county, music, poetry, rhetoric, mime, painting, sculpture, and architecture. In music the academic exponent of art concerns himself with the metaphysical half, the censor, the performer and the programme-builder with the physical half.

So much is clear enough ; but we must add another point to which Christian and pre-Christian thought gives the clue, namely that the two great kingdoms are not precisely collateral. There is a *logical priority* in the metaphysical kingdom. Movement is always, in the first place, *from* the metaphysical *to* the physical. Plato's " forms " and the medieval philosopher's " universals " are pre-existent ; they are pre-supposed by the phenomenal world. Christians say that " He came down from heaven ",[1] and that " Herein is love, not that we loved God, but that He loved us ".[2] We assume that " being " is prior to " living " and we are directed by Christian philosophy to believe that Truth is prior to Love and Ethics.[3] This priority, this fact that movement is in the first instance from the metaphysical to the physical and not contrariwise, is faithfully reflected in art. Art is essentially *communication*, and the communication is from the metaphysical to that part of the physical which is the affective region of man's consciousness. The fact that it reaches the affective as well as the rational consciousness is expressed when we say that it is an inseparable property of art to be *rhetorical*. This movement in music and in all art, then, is derived from the universal movement from the One to the Many, the metaphysical to the physical, which demands a responsive movement from mankind towards the metaphysical, but without which that response is impossible. Primitive human experience established at once the affective qualities of music ; the religious music of primitive peoples to which we referred on our opening pages is the music of people conscious that they are being in a sense acted upon from without. Conversely the earliest human abstract speculation on music established it equally certainly in the mathematical regions of metaphysics. Music to the Pythagoreans was virtually a quality of the

[1] The Nicene Creed.

[2] I John iv. 10.

[3] " In us, as in God, Love must proceed from the Word ". Jacques and Raissa Maritain, *Prayer and Intelligence* (a translation (1942) of *La Vie d'Oraison*, based on St. Thomas Aquinas), p. 1.

universe waiting to be discovered. In neither case is music in any sense a " human invention ".

Now the purpose of these descriptions and definitions is to lay before the reader the material upon which he makes a moral judgment every time he says " this music is good ". Dismissing as irrelevant and beneath notice the vulgar method of criticism which equates that expression with "this pleases me ", we may say that " good " music is that music which successfully establishes the required communication between the metaphysical and the physical kingdoms. Now there are three things which can prevent this success, namely, bad technique, bad use, and bad argument, and these correspond to failure in the legislatures of the three "county-towns."

By bad technique, or a failure in the metaphysical area, we mean those origins of simple ugliness which are abstracted by grammarians and theorists from the dispassionate examination of the beautiful—false harmonic progressions, bad instrumentation, and all the other errors against which the students of our academies are properly warned. By bad " use ", or failure in the physical area, we mean both such incongruities as merry music at funerals or bad programme-building, and also simple bad playing or singing. Bad argument, however, is a failure in the specifically rhetorical function of music, and corresponds to that incoherence or disregard of the auditor's necessities which makes a bad speech or a bad sermon. It happens that while our academies give much attention to the first of the three sources of error, and, as we have seen, our ecclesiastics and moralists have in the past attended carefully to the

second, the importance of the third and more fundamental error has hardly yet been recognised at all.
The analytical technique of the Viennese musical
theorist, Heinrich Schenker,[1] however, has opened up
the possibility of exposing bad argument in music,
and the work of Professor Donald Tovey was always
distinguished for the emphasis he laid not only on the
grammar but also on the syntax and rhetorical
technique of music.

The distinction which belongs to Augustine is,
however, that he alone succeeded in not only taking
the enquiry a step further but also in providing a
reasoned Christian answer to it, He asked the
fateful question, Whence come these failures in the
various strata of music ? We have noted as familiar
to all readers the efficient cause of the failure of some
music to fulfil its function of communicating the
metaphysical to the physical, but what of its first
cause ? The answer which Augustine gives, and
which we here propose to fit into the aesthetic scheme
we are constructing, is that the whole of the area we
have called " physical " is subject to that failure in
human nature called by Christians " sin ". " Original
sin " is a technical term of Christian theology meaning
that mankind is predisposed towards disobedience
by nature, and its implication is that he can be disposed
to obedience and goodness only by an act of will made
possible by grace, which is itself a character not of
man but of God. The allied doctrine of " total
depravity ", greatly scorned and abused by some, is
theological " shorthand " for the truth that there is no
activity of man which is exempt from this influence

[1] See Appendix B.

towards evil, no activity which does not require the addition of grace from God to bring it to perfection. Now music in its affective region, but not in its metaphysical, is an activity of mankind and therefore falls under the influence of sin. In its metaphysical aspect music is no more affected by sin than mathematics; once touched by human hands, it can *go wrong*.

Now sin is ultimately not reprehensible action or failure in goodness, but confusion and nonsense. Christian teaching has always held that view. It was prepared by the ethical thought of the Jews of the Old Testament, to whom the cardinal sin was idolatry ; idolatry is placing a created thing where God alone has the right to be. It is, in fact, human tampering with the divine order, or humanly introduced confusion. And the sin against the Holy Ghost, for which there is no forgiveness is primarily a metaphysical sin ; it is not lust or avarice or greed, but it is the deliberate choice of abstract evil ; it is saying " Evil, be thou my good ". The Evil Spirit in Goethe's *Faust* says, " I am the Spirit that denies " ; the Skeleton in Charles Williams's *Thomas Cranmer*,[1] in answer to Cranmer's " God, without whom nothing is strong ", says " I am the nothing you meant. I am sent to gather you into that nothing." The allegory of Eden teaches that the central core of sin is *disobedience*, the impatient tampering with the order laid down by God. Translated into philosophical terms this means that the origin of all error is the arbitrary tampering with metaphysical categories, the reversal of that which is " given " ; this is the metaphysical equivalent of man declaring that he is as God, competent not only to

---

[1] *Thomas Cranmer of Canterbury*, Oxford (1937), p. 46.

know but also to decide what shall be good and what evil, what sense and what nonsense.

When we dealt with the nineteenth century we discovered a notable capacity in the men of that age for ignoring final causes, for treating things not as " things in themselves " having a purpose of their own which man was required to respect, but as entirely subordinate to man's will.   Music, like many other things, was robbed of its final cause ; it had, in the hands of the commercial and the unscrupulous, no end of its own ; it was to be used for the adornment of man's life and the glorification of his prowess.   In as much as it was thus subjected it lost its individuality and its integrity and became a tool.   To deal in this way with one's neighbour is commonly called an act of pride ; but " pride " or *superbia* in medieval Christian spiritual teaching is not confined to the sphere of personal relationships.   It is the cardinal (or in modern jargon we should say " pivotal ") sin.   Thus Augustine expounded the cause of bad music as *superbia*.[2]   And in fact experience shows that careless writing, shoddy performance, wrong use, and lack of rational integrity in music or any other art is to be traced to this one source at last.   The anxiety to have a completed piece of work is the temptation which draws aside all but the greatest composers and performers from their duty of attending to every finest detail ; the temptation to glorify himself in a finished creation distracts the maker from his duty of courtesy towards his material.   The answer, then, to the root cause of bad music is the negation of disobedience and pride, namely, in the words of another Christian

[2] See Chapter II.

teacher, " courtesy ", or in the words of the Bible,
" penitence ".

This amounts to saying that a sound criticism of
music must take account of the legislature not only of
the three " county towns ", technique, art, and
aesthetic, but also of an imperial seat of justice and
origin of order, which is theology. Theology is the
science which has something to say of all other sciences,
which oversees both the metaphysical and the physical
kingdoms, and which alone can dispense justice and
establish order between them. Theological criticism
alone is universal criticism.

This we say with confidence, but we add, that we
may not be misunderstood, that being in the narrow
sense an expert in theology (that is, a student of the
literature or the dogma or the institutions of the
historical church) is in no way a qualification for
sound musical criticism. All the knowledge of music
that the best of critics and experts has ever had is
needed ; all the recognition of and respect for musical
metaphysics must be present. But to them must be
added a philosophy of criticism which is founded in
Christian theology. We must ask all the old questions
Is it well-made ? Is it suitable ? Is it coherent
in argument ? But to them we add the conviction
that only under Grace can music be brought to perfection. Criticism which stops short of a Christian
universality is merely negation ; it can only say what
is wrong, having no positive clue to the right. Such
negation is necessary, even as bye-laws are necessary,
to defend the musical kingdom from chaos. But bye-
laws are not enough to preserve a whole Empire from
chaos. Criticism by ecclesiastics which proceeds from

ground having not a square foot in common with that
from which technical musicians proceed may defend
the church from improprieties, but it does not promote
sympathy between the ecclesiastic and the musician.
It leads to the state of unarmed hostility and incom-
prehension which prevails to-day ; under this
dispensation the musician sees the ecclesiastic as a
pedant or a puritan, and the ecclesiastic sees the
musician as an incorrigible highbrow. But both
musician and ecclesiastic are men, and therefore subject
to the universal and imperial law enjoining just and
honourable thought and conduct ; more—and this
is the Christian's unique message—both are subject
to the imperial edict of Grace. Christian criticism
cannot make a bad piece of music good any more than
it can make a bad action good ; but the Grace of God
can make a sinner whole and can make a composer
better able to play his craft in all its complexity.

Judgment in the present situation (1967)

The only difficulty about that kind of judgment is
that what Christians call the grace of God may well
be something which a musician neither understands
nor acknowledges. Musicians do not speak that kind
of language. Musicians are musicians, not theologians.
In order that a Christian judgment about music may
become anything more than a word thrown to the
winds, satisfactory to the utterer but finding no
attentive ear, the Christian must have some understanding of what it means to be an artist.

Now a school of church music can do a great deal
of effective work in helping church musicians to make
better music : by instructing them in liturgy, in

music-history, in choir-training and organ playing, and in all the disciplines which church music acknowledges. But it is well known that academies of church music—of which there are two famous ones in Great Britain, and a very large number associated with American universities—are liable either to turn out musicians who have carefully laid aside any theological insights they may have had, and who therefore live entirely within the world of music and do no harm to anybody, or to turn out musicians who show no sympathy or patience with any but the most refined and recondite forms of church music. What they do not do, because at present they do not regard it as within their field (but where else is it if not there ?), is to create a forum in which the theologian can " find himself " as an artist, and the artist can " find himself " as a theologian. Church musicians, if they have any theology at all, are often naive to an alarming degree. Theologians are dogmatic to an offensive degree. Protestant traditions have tended to exalt theology as a science and to depress the status of the artist ; but theology is not a science. Its practice can never be wholly divorced from art. Theology can never be adequately expressed otherwise than in such poetry as " The Word was made flesh ". But theologians, especially on the Protestant side, are unwilling to admit this. Still worse, they are too ready to regard themselves as lawgivers—and that was the error which the earlier chapters of this essay exposed. For a Christian judgment to find its mark, it must be made by a Christian who sees the arts not as an ornament of life but as part of the fabric of life ; who sees the artist not as a man paid to amuse the idle but as the twentieth century equivalent of the prophet of the Old Testament.

The reason why it is possible to say this now, and possibly only now, is because the artist has forced his way into the centre of the stage of culture. He has always been well to one side or the other—either a paid entertainer of the very wealthy or a depressed exponent of popular folklore. The much-despised modern phenomenon of mass-art, from Promenade Concerts to the commercialized pop-market, has brought every kind of artist into the centre of public recognition, not least the musicians. Even theologians have been unable any longer to ignore the artist's existence. Pop-art may have its depraved and vulgar aspects, but it has made conversation between artists and theologians (as between artists and other kinds of people) not only possible but urgently necessary. Therefore it is right to capitalize on the simple fact, which old-fashioned church people still refer to with rueful regret, that the film star stands now where the popular preacher stood three generations ago. We may not like this very much : we may justly claim that the old preacher compared pretty favourably with the film-star in his grasp of the meaning of life and his ability to conduct himself with sanity and sense : we may claim with equal justice that the cathedral organist is not self-evidently a worse musician than the jazz trumpeter or the much idolized pop-singer. But if what everybody is listening to nowadays is the television star, who is bound to be in some sense an artist, not the preacher, who has preferred not to be thought an artist, then it is the more obvious that the professional Christian must hasten to find common ground with the artist wherever the artist is at present standing. And this common ground will not be hard to find. The more crowded the world is, the more ground you must share with your neighbour, and it is the crowdedness of the modern world, in which everybody knows everybody else's business, that makes it necessary for the theologian, having done his thinking and seen his visions, to open conversation with the artist. There can be nothing remote now about theology.

But that need not mean that either the theologian or the artist must lose his integrity. The theologian should retain his advantage of being trained in clear thought ; the artist will be wise not to adopt a cynical or solipsistic pose. If both recognize their common humanity—both are men, both are capable of error, both are at their worst when they are alone—then the conversation will continue, and will make sense. In the matter of musical judgment, what will happen will be that the theologian, readily able to distinguish levels of judgment, will not want any more to say that all Victorian music is bad, or all jazz music is bad, or all " pop " music is bad, or all sixteenth century poly-phonic music is good. He will ask in what ways music of any style can be brought into harmony with the truth that he wants conveyed : and also in what ways his own methods of communication of that truth can be helped, improved, modified and rebuked by the artist.

Conversation is the heart of it. This is the age in which it can happen.

QUOTATIONS FROM THE FATHERS AND AUTHORITIES OF THE EARLY AND MEDIEVAL CHURCH

✣ I ✣

ORIGEN (c. 185–254), commenting on Psalm 150 :

" ' Praise Him upon the psaltery and harp.
Praise Him with the timbrel and dance :
Praise Him with stringed instruments and organs.
Praise Him upon the loud cymbals :
Praise Him upon the high-sounding cymbals.'

The harp (*cithara*) is the active soul, which is moved by Christ's commands. The timbrel (*tympanum*) is the mortification of natural desire by moral rectitude. The dance (*chorus*) is the unison of rational souls speaking the same words together, forgetting their differences. The stringed instruments (*chordae*) represent the agreement between the music of instruments and the music of virtue. The organ (*organum*) is the Church of God, consisting of souls contemplative and active. The 'loud' cymbal (*benesonans*) is the active soul made prisoner by the desire for Christ ; the 'high-sounding' cymbal (*iubilationis*) is the pure mind informed by Christ's salvation."

(From the Commentary on Psalm 150 : 3b-5.
Migne, *P.G.* XII. 1683.[1]

✣ 2 ✣

The same author commenting on Jeremiah iv. 5 :

" ' Declare ye in Judah, and publish in Jerusalem, and say, Blow ye the trumpet in the land. . . .'
Divine speech, bracing the hearer and equipping him for war against the unruly passions and against the enemies of virtue, equipping him also for the heavenly feast (for it is to be understood in both senses) is always the interpretation of the *trumpet* in scripture."

(*P.G.* XIII. 319.)

[1] References in this form are to Migne's *Patrologia Graeca* and *Patrologia Latina*, volume and column.

Appendices

∽ 3 ∾

LACTANTIUS (b. 290) on the true pleasure of Christian music.

" The man who is concerned for the truth, and who would
avoid self-deception, must set aside all those dangerous and
harmful pleasures which may enslave his soul as sweet foods
may enslave his body. He must prefer the true to the
illusive, the eternal to the transitory, the beneficial to the
merely pleasant. Nothing will delight your sight except
what you see to be essentially good and right. Nothing will
please your ears but what nourishes your soul and tends to
your improvement. Above all it is forbidden to pervert to
evil purposes that sense which is given us for the purpose of
apprehending the divine teaching. So, if it is pleasure to
hear music, let your best pleasure be to sing and hear the
praises of God. That is true pleasure which is the familiar
friend of virtue."

De Vero Cultu 6:21. (*P.L.* VI. 714.)

∽ 4 ∾

EUSEBIUS OF CAESAREA (c. 265–340) the author of the celebrated *Ecclesiastical History*, writes in his commentaries
in praise of congregational psalmody.

From the Commentary on Psalm lxv (lxvi). 1-2 :
" ' Make a joyful noise unto God, all ye lands :
Sing forth the honour of his name ; make his praise
to be glorious. . . .''
This Psalm is as evangelical as the preceding ; it treats of
the calling of the gentiles. Therefore it enjoins the whole
earth, that is, all the inhabitants of the globe, not to bow
down to the grievous joke of the Mosaic law, but to perform
only those duties celebrated in this present psalm, namely,
to rejoice in God, to sing to his name, to give praise to his
glory, and to say to him, ' *How terrible are thy works* ' and
' *Through the greatness of thy power thine enemies shall
submit themselves unto thee* '.''

(*P.G.* XXIII. 647.)

(This is part of a long passage expounding many Biblical
texts in praise of psalmody. Cf. *Comm.* Ps. lxv. 7-9 ;
(*P.G.* XXIII. 658.)

Appendices

◦ 5 ◦

From the *Commentary* on Psalm xci (xcii). 2-3.

" ' To shew forth thy lovingkindness in the morning
    And thy faithfulness every night
  Upon an instrument of ten strings and upon the psaltery :
    Upon the harp with a solemn sound.''

This passage bids us rehearse the divine truth at the break
of day, having kept our souls and bodies holy and unstained
by any impurity during the night-season, and in the hours
of evening to take up our devotions again, making mention
of God. For when in days gone by the peoples of the
Circumcision worshipped God by types and figures, it was
appropriate that they should sing the praises of God with
psaltery and harp, and indeed that they should show forth
that same praise on the Sabbath day, even though in so
doing they encroached on the day's leisure and so broke the
law. Now when we read this in the Apostle—

  ' To be a Jew is not to be a Jew outwardly ; to be circum-
    cised is not to be circumcised outwardly, in the flesh.
    He is a Jew indeed who is one inwardly ; true circum-
    cision is achieved in the heart, according to the spirit,
    not the letter of the law, for God's, not for man's
    approval '[1]

we can say that we are in this fashion ' Jews inwardly '
when we sing God's praise in spiritual songs, with a living
psaltery and an ensouled harp. The measure of God's
acceptance of the singing of a Christian congregation, and
of his delight in it, is the unanimity of mind, passion and
sentiment, the unity of faith and piety with which we sing
together the melodies of our praises. The same apostle
commands us to exhort one another in ' psalms and hymns
and spiritual music '[2] ; here then is the spiritual psalmody,
the spiritual harp in our worship. Another line of thought
shows the harp as the symbol of the whole body, by whose
movements and actions the soul pours out worthy praise to
God. The ten-stringed psaltery, by the same token, is the
worship of a sanctified spirit through the five senses of the

---

[1] Romans ii. 28-9. Translation of Mgr. Ronald Knox.
[2] Ephesians v. 19 (Knox).

234

body and the five virtues of the soul; upon which the
same apostle says 'I mean to use mind as well as spirit
when I offer prayer, use mind as well as spirit when I sing
psalms '."[2]

◇ 6 ◇

ATHANASIUS (295–373), in a spiritual tract, gives a hint of the
use of psalmody in the private devotion of Christians
in the fourth century.

" At midnight thou shall arise and sing praise to the Lord
thy God.   For in this same hour did our Lord rise from the
dead, and sang praise to his Father.   On this account it is
ordained that we praise God at this hour. . . . Say as many
psalms as thou canst say standing. . . . After three psalms
say ' Alleluia ! '."

De Virginitate 20 (P.G. XXVIII. 275.)

◇ 7 ◇

THE CAPPADOCIAN FATHERS make characteristic contributions
to this subject.   BASIL OF CAESAREA (c. 330–379), the
philosopher, writes at length ; GREGORY OF NYSSA (c. 335–
94), the preacher, has one comment: GREGORY NAZIANZEN
(c. 329–80), the poet-brother of Basil, writes some of the
earliest hymns.   BASIL in a sermon enjoins the use of
psalmody.
" If any man does not fall in immediately with the
practice of psalmody, let him not associate himself with the
sentiments of him who said ' How sweet are thy words unto
my taste !   Yea, sweeter than honey to my mouth !' ;
nor may he think his slothfulness to be a great danger to
the church.   He must mend his ways or be expelled, for a
little leaven must not be allowed to corrupt the whole
mass."

Sermon I.5.   (P.G. XXXII. 1145.)

---

[2] I Corinthians xiv. 15 (Knox).

235

Appendices

✑ 8 ✑

In the same sermon, Basil speaks of the persuasive effects of music.

" God mingles the sweetness of harmony with the divine Truth so that while we are enjoying the pleasures of hearing the music we may unconsciously gather up the benefits of the words which are being spoken. This is just what a wise doctor will do when, obliged to give bitter medicine to a sick man, he lines the medicine-cup with honey. The skilful harmonies of the psalms are worked out for our benefit, so that we, who are young in years or at any rate immature in character, may in the act of singing be in fact taming the uncouthness of our spirits."

Sermon I. 3. (*P.G.* XXXII. 1135.)

✑ 9 ✑

At the beginning of his *Commentary* on the Psalms, Basil mentions the " spiritual " quality of the psaltery, which he considers the appropriate instrument for music in worship.

" I am sure that in the music of the psaltery grace from the Holy Spirit is conveyed, and for this reason, that in this alone of all musical instruments does the sound proceed from a *higher* part of the instrument. The metal of the lyre and harp produces the sound, when they are played, from *below* ; but the psaltery draws its seemly modulations from its higher part. This symbolises very aptly the obligation which we have to seek diligently those things which are above, and not to be drawn away by pleasant sounds to the sordid concerns of the flesh."

Homilia in Psalmos, ad init. (*P.G.* XXIX. 214.)

Compare for defences of Psalmody and teaching on the use of music in worship. *De Legendis Libris Gentilium* 5-7 (*P.G.* XXXI. 578-583) and *Epist. Class.* II. 207. 3 (*P.G.* XXXII. 763).

GREGORY OF NYSSA writes in approval of hymnody, as being a part of the essential " harmony of the universe " in his *Commentarium in Psalmos* III. (*P.G.* XLIV. 442.)

For a hymn by GREGORY NAZIANZEN, translated into English, see Brownlie, *Hymns of the Eastern Church* (1913), p. 20, and *Revised Church Hymnary* (1927), No. 458.

Appendices

AMBROSE (c. 333–397), the writer and inspirer of the earliest
Latin hymnody praises psalmody as a means to unity in
the Church.

" What a labour it is to achieve silence in church while
the Lessons are being read. When one man would speak,
the congregation makes a disturbance. But when the
psalm is read[1] it makes its own ' silence ', since all are
speaking and there is no disturbance. Psalms are sung
by emperors ; the common people rejoice in them. Each
man does his utmost in singing what will be a blessing to all.
Psalms are sung in the home and rehearsed on the streets.
A psalm is learnt without labour and remembered with
delight. Psalmody unites those who disagree, makes
friends of those at odds, brings together those who are
out of charity with one another. Who could retain a
grievance against the man with whom he had joined in
singing before God ? The singing of praise is the very
bond of unity, when the whole people join in song a single
act of song. The strings of the harp are of varying lengths,
but the harmony is a unity. The musician's fingers, too,
may often make mistakes on the small strings, but in the
congregation that great Musician, the Spirit, cannot err.
Psalmody is the rewarding work of the night, the grateful
relaxation of the busy day, the good beginning and the
fortifying conclusion of all work. It is the ministry of
the angels, the strength of the heavenly host, the spiritual
sacrifice."

In Psalm i *Enarratio* 9.   (*P.L.* XIV. 925.)

For the same line of thought, compare *Hexaemeron* III. 23.
(*P.L.* XIV. 165.)

In another Psalm-commentary Ambrose writes of the elevating
powers of psalmody.

---

[1] The same word (*Leguntur*) is used here as in the previous sentence.
But it must here mean " sung " rather than " read ". Singing was,
after all, still very near to reading.

" The man who speaks[1] a hymn of praise speaks spiritually
and with a pure heart, shutting out every kind of human
passion. His devotion is hampered by no heaviness,
disturbed by no bitterness of grief. He continues singing
beyond all passion and distraction the hymn while God
speaks."

In Ps. xliv (xlv). 9. (P.L. XIV. 1101.)

◌ 12 ◌

In a spiritual tract Ambrose denounces those who prefer
secular music to the spiritual blessings of sacred music.

" And so it is justly said, ' Woe unto them that rise up
early in the morning and follow strong drink,'[2] when they
ought to be rendering praises to God ; for this should they
rise before the dawn and run to meet the Sun of righteous-
ness,[3], who visits his own and arises upon us if we have
bestirred ourselves for the sake of Christ and not of wine
and luxury. They are singing hymns—will you cling to
your harp ? They are singing psalms ; what business have
you with a psaltery and a drum ? Woe indeed to you for
abandoning your salvation and choosing death.[4]"

De Elia et Jejunio, 55. (P.L. XIV. 717).

◌ 13 ◌

JOHN CHRYSOSTOM (344–407) loses no opportunity of passionately denouncing the theatre and all its works. He therefore makes many derogatory remarks concerning music.
But he never urges the abandonment of sacred music by
Christians. This is Chrysostom's description of the contemporary theatre :

" The habitation of pestilence, the gymnasium of licence,
the school of profligacy."

De Poenitentia VI ad init. (P.G. II. 314.)

[1] Here again Ambrose uses a neutral word, this time *dicit*, to express
what we must understand to be " singing ".

[2] This passage, like much of Ambrose, is full of allusions to Scripture.
Here he quotes Isa. v. 11.

[3] Malachi iv. 2.

[4] Deut. xxx. 19.

238

✑ 14 ✑

And again—
"Surely you can see the enfeebling effect the theatre has
upon its audiences?"

In *S. Barbanum Martyrem,* 4. (*P.G.* II. 682.)

✑ 15 ✑

"He who walks near a precipice, even though he does not
fall immediately, trembles, and often through that very
trembling is caused to fall. . . . He who stares at the bodies
of others, although he does not commit adultery, is none the
less guilty of lust, and according to the word of Christ is
become an adulterer."

Ad Antiochenos Homilia 15:4. (*P.G.* II. 159.)

✑ 16 ✑

Here Chrysostom speaks of the sobering effect of a national
disaster:
"How many words have we spent in admonishing this
idle multitude and advising them to avoid the theatres and
the licence that they generate? But they have not
abstained; on the contrary, up to this very day they have
continued to run after dancing-shows, choosing the devil's
conversation rather than that which stands in the fulness of
God's Church. So the clamour of the theatres has drowned
the psalmody of the Church. . . .
But now behold, without a word from us, (for we have
said nothing of this), they have of their own accord shut up
the dance-hall, and the circus is deserted. Before this
many of our own people frequented these performances,
but now they are all fled into the church for refuge, and are
singing praises, all of them, to our God. . . . Truly grief
is more profitable than laughter."

Ib. 15:1. (*P.G.* II. 152-3.)

✑ 17 ✑

Chrysostom has no hesitation in conceding the power of music:
"Thus does the devil stealthily set fire to the city. It

is not a matter of running up ladders and using petroleum or pitch or tow ; he uses things far more pernicious—lewd sights, base speech, degraded[1] music, and songs full of all kinds of wickedness."

De Poenitentia VI. (*P.G.* II.315.)

⌁ 18 ⌁

" But keep silent, and listen attentively. In the theatre, when the chorus sings its devilish ditties, there is great silence, in order that these pernicious tunes may make their impression. That chorus consists of mimics and dancers, led by some player of the cithara ; they sing some devilish and damnable song, and he who sings is the spirit of wickedness and damnation. Here on the other hand, where the chorus consists of pious men and the chorus-master is the Prophet, and the tune is not of satanic agency, but of the Grace of the Spirit, and he who is praised is not the devil, but God—surely here it is our duty to keep a great silence, and to listen with great trembling."

From the *Commentary* on Psalm 8. (*P.G.* V. 106.)
(Compare Basil, Homily IV in Hexaemeron, I.

P.G. XXIX. 81.)

⌁ 19 ⌁

JULIAN THE APOSTATE (361–363), the last imperial persecutor of Christianity, whose attempt to restore paganism fifty years after Constantine's edict of Milan was the fruit of a religious patriotism as genuine as that of Marcus Aurelius, writes thus concerning the theatre, giving unexpected confirmation to the Christian view expressed in the writings of Chrysostom :

" No priest should, in any place, attend these licentious theatrical shows . . . nor introduce (an actor) into his own house, for that is altogether unfitting. Indeed, if it were possible to expel such shows completely from the theatres and give back a pure stage to Dionysus I should certainly have attempted zealously to carry this out ; but

---

[1] διακεκλασμένα.

since I thought that this was impossible, and that even if it were possible it would, for other reasons, not be expedient, I abstained entirely from this ambition. I do expect, however, that priests should withdraw themselves from the obscenity of the theatres and leave them to the crowd. . . ." *Ep.* 89.6.

(This is part of a quotation which appears in Wellesz, *A History of Byzantine Music and Hymnography* (1949), page 73, and is reproduced here by kind permission of the author).

☞ 20 ☞

AUGUSTINE has already been referred to as one of the great musical thinkers of all time. Elsewhere, however, than in *De Musica* (for which see Chapter II) he often refers to music, and his comments are always characteristic.

Three passages from the *Confessions*[1] follow.

" The pleasures of the ear did indeed draw me and hold me more tenaciously, but You have set me free. Yet still when I hear those airs, in which Your words breathe life, sung with sweet and measured voice, I do, I admit, find a certain satisfaction in them, yet not such as to grip me too close, for I can depart when I will. Yet in that they are received into me along with the truths which give them life, such airs seek in my heart a place of no small honour, and I find it hard to know what is their due place. At times indeed it seems to me that I am paying them greater honour than is their due—when, for example, I feel that by those holy words my mind is kindled more religiously and fervently to a flame of piety because I hear them sung than if they were not sung : and I observe that all the varying emotions of my spirit have modes proper to them in voice and song whereby, by some secret affinity, they are made more alive. It is not good that the mind should be enenervated by this bodily pleasure. But it often ensnares me, in that the bodily sense does not accompany the reason as following after it in proper order, but having been admitted to aid the reason, strives to run before and take the lead. In this matter I sin unawares, and then grow aware.

[1] Translation of F. J. Sheed (1943), by permission.

Yet there are times when through too great a fear of this temptation, I err in the direction of over-severity—even to the point sometimes of wishing that the melody of all the lovely airs with which David's Psalter is commonly sung should be banished not only from my own ears, but from the Church's as well : and that seems to me a safer course, which I remember often to have heard told of Athanasius, bishop of Alexandria, who had the reader of the psalm utter it with so little modulation of the voice that he seemed to be saying it rather than singing it. Yet when I remember the tears I shed, moved by the songs of the Church in the early days of my new faith : and again when I see that I am moved not by the singing but by the things that are sung—when they are sung with a clear voice and proper modulation—I recognise once more the usefulness of this practice. Thus I fluctuate between the peril of indulgence and the profit I have found : and on the whole I am in-clined—though I am not propounding any irrevocable opinion—to approve the custom of singing in Church, that by the pleasure of the ear the weaker minds may be roused to a feeling of devotion. Yet whenever it happens that I am more moved by the singing than by the thing that is sung, I admit that I have grievously sinned, and then I should wish rather not to have heard the singing."

Confessions X. 33. (*P.L.* XXXII. 799 f.)

༄ 21 ༄

" The days were not long enough as I meditated, and found wonderful delight in meditating, upon the depth of Your design for the salvation of the human race. I wept at the beauty of Your hymns and canticles, and was power-fully moved at the sweet sound of Your Church's singing. These sounds flowed into my ears, and the truth streamed into my heart: so that my feeling of devotion overflowed, and the tears ran from my eyes, and I was happy in them."

Ib. IX. 6, ad fin.

༄ 22 ༄

" It was only a little while before that the church of

Milan had begun to practise this kind of consolation and exultation, to the great joy of the brethren singing together with heart and voice. For it was only about a year, or not much more, since Justina, the mother of the boy emperor Valentinian, was persecuting Ambrose in the interests of her own heresy : for she had been seduced by the Arians. The devoted people had stayed day and night in the church, ready to die with the bishop, Your servant. And my mother, Your handmaid, bearing a great part of the trouble and vigil, had lived in prayer. I also, though still not warmed by the fire of Your Spirit, was stirred to excitement by the disturbed and wrought-up state of the city. It was at this time that the practice was instituted of singing hymns and psalms after the manner of the Eastern Churches, to keep the people from being altogether worn out with anxiety and want of sleep. The custom has been retained from that day to this, and has been imitated by many, indeed in almost all congregations throughout the world."

Ib. IX. 7, ad init.

ᴏ 23 ᴏ

Boethius (St. Severinus) (480–524) writes in his treatise *De Musica* of the essential character of music.

"From these arguments four chief branches of learning are established. The other three are directed towards the search for truth, but music is associated not only with the speculative but also with the moral activities. Nothing is more characteristic of human nature than its capacity for being soothed by sweet music and braced by strong music. This is not true only of specialists or confined to any particular age. It is found in studies of all kinds, and as for ages, musical modes are so naturally and spontaneously associated with certain passions that there is no age, whether infancy, youth, or dotage, which remains unmoved by the sound of a pleasant melody. So we may conclude that Plato was right when he said that the soul of the universe is informed by a harmony essentially musical. Compare the harmony and compactness of the human body with that harmony and compactness which delights us in music, and you will see that the harmonies of music and of humanity are one and the same in their characteristic "similtude". Similitude is agreeable, dissimilitude disagreeable and odious. From this arise the differences between one character and another. The irresponsible mind delights in the irresponsible modes, and by frequent hearing of them is corrupted until it is finally destroyed. Conversely, the more spirited mind prefers the spirited modes, and by them is confirmed in its own character. That is why each musical mode is distinguished by the name of a nation, such as Lydian and Phrygian. Each mode is named after that nation to which it is especially appropriate. For a nation prefers those modes which accord with its character. It is impossible that the softer modes should appeal to hardy peoples, or the harsher modes to men of gentle character. The foundation and preservative of all love and pleasure is, as has been said, similitude. Therefore Plato thinks that we must take the greatest care to see that once music is established in a good tradition, changes do not creep in. He says, indeed, that nothing will be as certain to corrupt a community than the gradual weaning away of its members from sober and well-disciplined music."

De Musica I. (*P.L.* LXIII. 1167 ff, Cf. 1170 f.)

♫ 24 ♫

CASSIODORUS (485–580) writes to Boethius. Most of his extensive work on music is derivative, but in this passage he takes a more liberal line than that which Boethius inherits from Plato.

"The Dorian mode spread abroad modesty and the increase of chastity ; the Phrygian excites men to battle and fans the flames of wrath. The Aeolian assuages the storms of the mind and gives sleep to those whom it has soothed ; the Ionian sharpens blunt wits and ministers to those weighed down by earthly cares, giving them a heavenly desire for good ; the Lydian is a defence against the oppression of idleness and boredom, fortifies the weakening and strengthens them by its sweetness. By using these to

evil ends, our corrupt world causes the label "Poison" to
be set upon an honest medicine.[1]"

From the Epistle to Boethius. (*P.L.* LXIX. 571.)
Cf. the *Commentary* on Psalm 98 (*P.L.* LXX. 692) and
De Musica (*P.L.* LXX. 1209 ff.).

✎ 25 ✎

ISIDORUS (570–636) reminds the reader that the practice of
writing music down was still unknown in his time.

"The audible sound of music flows away into the past
and as it passes is impressed on the memory; hence the
poetic tradition that the Muses are the daughters of Jupiter
and Memoria. For except the sounds be retained in the
memory of men they perish, for it is impossible to write
them down."

Etymologia 3-15. (*P.L.* LXXXII. 163.)

✎ 26 ✎

The same author gives music the praise that has become
conventional—the legacy of Platonism.

"Without music no training is complete, for none can
be separated from it. The universe is said to be composed
of a certain "harmony" of sounds and the heaven revolves
under the direction of harmonic authority. Music exalts
the passions and guides the senses into different habits.
In battle the sound of the trumpet kindles the fighters;
and the louder the blast, the bolder becomes the fighting
spirit. Oarsmen are heartened by shanties, and music
makes the mind better able to endure all manner of hard
labour."

Ib. 3-17. (*P.L.* LXXXII. 164.)

✎ 27 ✎

AGOBARD OF LYONS (779–840), in a treatise on the Correction
of the Antiphonary, makes certain criticisms of contemporary usages. He reproves the disagreeable custom of
choosing church dignitaries for their good voices.

"Note how the apostolic Father [*sc.* Gregory I] rebukes

---

[1] *honestum remedium turpe fecit esse commentum.*

245

the custom by which the offices of cantor and deacon were combined ; he says that in deacons one should look for purity of living, not sweetness of voice. . . . Having condemned this custom he gives it as his opinion that psalms and other lections should be pronounced by sub-deacons or by clergy of the minor orders ; only the duty of reading the Gospels should be assigned to the deacon. This makes it clear that in those days psalms were commonly sung in church, and it remains the general view that they, rather than the compositions of this or that poet, should constitute the chief part in the offices of divine worship : such compositions, by the way, no one who knows anything of his unblemished faith and distinguished learning would dream of attributing to the Father himself."

De Correctione Antiphonarii, 15. (*P.L.* CIV. 336.)

∽ 28 ∽

His puritan tendencies are further exemplified earlier in the same treatise.

" We have therefore corrected the Antiphonary in such measure as our powers allow, removing what seemed to us to be trivial, misleading, or frankly blasphemous. We have, furthermore, frequently advised you to this effect, and have thought it necessary to include the chief matter of our admonition in the preface to this book in order to meet any complaints which our contemporaries or our posterity may see fit to prefer. We make no general enactment, but we offer what our mediocre intelligence permits for use in the house of God, whose care is given into our charge. We assume nothing on the authority of our own opinion, but we follow the authority of Scripture, the examples and institutions of the catholic Fathers, and the legislations of the sacred canons. . . ."

(An example of his policy :) . .

" Consider this expression—

' The Son of God came forth from his hidden dwelling to visit and console all who desire him with their whole heart.'

This we hold to be disfigured by the ineptitude of the words and the falsity and absurdity of the sentiment. It speaks with great irreverence of the ' dwelling ' of the Son, and the assertion that he visited and consoled all who desired him is far from the truth, which is that it was by his power alone that those whom he visited were enabled to recognise and desire him."

> *Ib.* 3 and 5. (*P.L.* CIV. 330-1.)
> Cf. *Ib.* 18-19. (*P.L.* CIV. 338.)

↶ 29 ↷

JOHANNES COTTO (*fl.* 1100), who alone of the authorities quoted here is not an ordained dignitary of the church, is none the less worth quoting for the view which he expresses concerning new music in the church. In his treatise *De Musica*, after giving the story of Saul and David as an example of the power of music, he continues :—

" Now since music has such power to act upon the minds of men, it was quite proper that it should be accepted in the holy Church. Its acceptance, indeed, began in the time of Saint Ignatius the martyr, and was greatly encouraged by Saint Ambrose of Milas. After this the most blessed Pope Gregory, acting, we are told, under the direct influence and at the dictation of the Holy Spirit, composed songs, and gave to the Roman Church hymns for the celebration of all the offices of the Church's year. . . . Well then, seeing that these hymns for the church's offices which we have mentioned were thus composed, and that we may add to them the compositions of certain others who have lived nearer to our own time, I see nothing to prevent the musicians of our own day making their contribution. New melodies may not indeed be necessary in the modern church, but may we not try our skill in setting some of the songs and the mournful poems of our own authors ? It is because we are both seeking and also (by assumption) granting this licence for new compositions that it seems proper to add some directions for the composition of music."

> (*P.L.* CL. 1414, 1417.)

(It will be observed that Cotto does not share Agobard's view on Gregory's compositions, nor does he accept the Platonic interdict on new compositions.)

Appendices

∽ 30 ∽

Under the headline " Concerning the Rejection of Inferior Usages ", the same author has this ; in which he qualifies his enthusiasm for innovation :

" We must mention certain songs, of long standing in church use, which are disfigured by their lack of melodic regularity, and must urge with all possible emphasis that this and every other kind of debased usage which has survived to our day be abolished. Our Lord delights, as we know, in the unity of faith, of baptism, and of character ; clearly, then, this complicated confusion of choral effects which the singers inflict upon us not under compulsion nor in ignorance but of deliberate choice, is a public offence. . . . In correcting these errors, therefore, we have used moderation, and have given such directions as, being slight, will not involve the readers in laborious exercise, and will, so far as new matter is concerned, stray as little as possible from the traditional path."

De Musica. (*P.L.* CL. 1425.)

∽ 31 ∽

JOHN OF SALISBURY (c. 1115–80) protests against part-singing in church.

" Could you but hear one of these enervating performances executed with all the devices of the art, you might think it a chorus of Sirens, but not of men, and you would be astonished at the singers' facility, with which indeed neither that of the nightingale or parrot, nor of whatever else there may be that is more remarkable in this kind, can compare. This facility is displayed in accents and discants, in the dividing or redoubling of the notes, in the repetition of phrases and the clashing of the voices, while in all this the high or even the highest notes of the scale are so mixed with the lower and the lowest, that the ears are almost deprived of their power to distinguish."

Polycraticus I. 6.

The edict of Pope John XXII, 1325. (The Latin text may be found in Friedberg, *Corpus Juris Canonici*, c. 1255 ff.)

" The learned authority of the Fathers of the Church directs that in the observances of divine praise which we offer in the discharge of our rightful service we may require of the worshipper an alert mind, of the speaker uninterrupted discourse, and of the singers a modest demeanour which expresses itself in grave and serene music. The Lord's song in their mouths sounded graciously ; indeed, when musicians so sing and utter their words that God is extolled in the heart and devotion to Him is kindled, the song cannot but be gracious. For this reason it is laid down that for the better devotion of the faithful there shall be psalmody in the church of God.

To this end, let priests and people sing the services of morning and evening, and the celebrations of the Mass, reverently, clearly, and to suitable music, finding their delight in good enunciation and their full satisfaction in musical propriety.

But there is a new school, whose disciples, observing with care the regularity of musical time-values, concern themselves with new devices, preferring their new inventions to the ancient songs of the church ; by their practices the music of the liturgies is disordered with semibreves, minims, and even shorter notes. They break up the melodies with hockets, they embellish them with discants ; sometimes they so force them out of shape with ' triples ' and other music proper to profane occasions that the principles of the antiphonary and the gradual are wholly neglected. They forget on what they are building ; they so disguise the melody that it becomes indistinguishable ; indeed the multitude of notes is so confusing that the seemly rise and decorous fall of the plainsong melody, which should be the distinguishing feature of the music, is entirely obscured. They run and will not rest, they inebriate the ears without soothing them ; the conduct of the singers is so appropriate to their matter that decent devotion is held in contempt and a reprehensible frivolity is paraded for admiration. Boethius is right when he says that the frivolous mind is

249

either delighted by hearing frivolous music or by the habit of attending to it is emasculated and corrupted.

Therefore we and our brethren have long held that this requires correction. We hasten to banish and eradicate this thing from the church of God. We will use all our power to destroy it. On the advice, then, of our brethren we emphatically enjoin that from this time no one shall presume to make use of such material, or any similar material, in the offices we have mentioned, especially during the canonical hours or in celebrating the solemnities of the Mass. If any disobey he shall be punished according to this canon by eight days' suspension from office. This punishment shall be administered either by the ordinaries in the place where the offence was committed or, where it is not a matter involving deprivation of office, by their deputies ; where deprivation is involved it shall be administered by the President or approved officer in whose hands the punishment of such offences and excesses shall be deemed to lie most fitly or by their deputies.

In this we do not mean to prohibit the use of harmony occasionally on festive days either in the celebration of the Mass or in the divine offices ; we approve such harmony as follows the melody at the intervals, for example, of the octave, fifth, and fourth, and such harmony as may be supported by the simple chant of the church ; but we prescribe this condition, that the integrity of the chant itself remain undamaged, and that no well-established piece of music is altered as under this authority. Such harmonies as fulfil these conditions we hold to be soothing to the ear, conducive to devotion, and a safeguard against inattention in the minds of those who sing psalms to God."

HEINRICH SCHENKER (1867–1935)

In case our observations on page 219 may seem to lack solidity we add here a note on the work of Heinrich Schenker as it affects our thesis. Schenker was a Viennese musical theorist who developed a scheme of analysis which we can best explain by analogy. If a piece of prose or a speech or a sermon is under criticism, it is possible to say of it that its grammar is bad or that it was inappropriate to the occasion for which it was designed. These roughly correspond to the two more familiar categories of musical criticism. It is also possible to complain that it does not say what it set out to say, that its argument is faulty. The most serviceable way in which to support such a criticism is to break down the material under review into a series of abstracts in *précis* form, each shorter than the former, until what was first seen as a continuous argument is found in reality to consist of a series of superimposed *strata* of argument. In relating these strata to each other, and in relating the basic points of the material to the foreground-material as it was originally presented by its author, gaps in the argument are readily exposed.

Such a method of abstracting the chief points of such material has not only a negative but also a positive service to render. It is often necessary for a reader or auditor to have some faculty which will enable him to distinguish what is peripheral from what is central. If he hears a statesman making a speech about socialism in which there occurs an illustration from pig-breeding, the intelligent auditor will recognise that an error in the technics of pig-breeding may not necessarily vitiate the general argument about socialism. It is a cardinal necessity in interpreting Scripture that the astronomy of the Psalms or the horticulture of the parables shall not be regarded as directly affecting the spiritual message they have to convey. The best defence against propaganda is the cultivation of precisely this faculty of discernment.

This faculty Schenker applies in a precisely analogous way to music, and his analyses have the effect of breaking a continuous piece of music down into *strata* of musical argument, by which means he can show not only the weakness of bad musical rhetoric but also the richness and elaboration of thought in great music.

Professor Tovey, though not an overt follower of Schenker (he does not mention his name in his published writings) followed the same general method when, for example, he wrote so scornfully of those who say that the Fifth Symphony of Beethoven is " built up on " a phrase of four notes ; to this he replies that on the contrary that work is built up on unusually long musical paragraphs. (*Essays in Musical Analysis*, Vol. I, p. 38 ff.) Again (*Essays in Musical Analysis, Chamber Music*, p. 169), in order to enable the hearer to seize the gist of the Handel theme on which Brahms wrote his Variations for Piano, Op. 25, Tovey gives a summary of the theme without its musical decorations which is exactly like a Schenker-stratum. His distinction in his analyses of works in sonata-form between " subjects " and " groups " (as one might distinguish between " points " and " paragraphs ") is only one of many other examples that could be adduced.

Schenker's work has received little recognition so far, partly because of the obscurity of the terms in which it is written, and partly because of an unfortunate and indeed offensive admixture of Nietzschean diction in the foreground of some of his teaching. This hasty distillation, however, while doing nothing like justice to Schenker's contribution,, contains, we believe, the important part of his contribution to musical thought. The reader may be referred to two sources in English for reading on Schenker : Adèle Katz, *Challenge to Musical Tradition* (Putnam, 1947), and Michael Mann, " Schenker's Contribution to Musical Theory," in *The Music Review*, vol. X, no. 1 (February, 1949), pp. 1 ff. Neither of these works is in our opinion wholly authoritative or without its misleading moments, but the bibliography in Mann's article is excellent and thoroughly reliable.

TABLE OF HYMN TUNES

Hymn tunes referred to in the text have their *Songs of Praise* reference numbers given in a footnote. The following table is for the use of those who have no access to *Songs of Praise*, and wish to consult the tunes in other books.

	EH[1]	A&M[2]	M[3]	CP[4]	CH[5]	H[6]	P[7]	M[8]
Beatitudo	—	528	605	2A	592	416	350	—
Behold Me Standing	—	—	331	—	—	—	—	—
Bishopthorpe	408	208	107	392	137	360	274	—
Diadem	—	—	6A	—	—	—	—	72
Dies Irae	—	—	398†	—	—	—	—	—
Dominus Regit Me	490	197	76	61	438	345	79	67
Dundee (French)	428	272	625	361	227	397	85	215
Easter Hymn	133	134	204	145	119	85	182	439
Ein' Feste Burg	362	183	494	485	526	551	363	20
Gerontius	—	185	74	71	32	343	—	—
Helmsley	7	51	264	160	160	5	—	—
Hursley	39A	24	942	—	413	166	50	254
Ilkley (Calm)	—	—	285	291	—	—	—	—
Innsbruck	278	34	946	629	284	181	53	—
Irish	504	263	503	585	153	444	—	56
Kent (Devonshire, Invitation)	347	71	496	395	225	—	—	350
King's Norton	419	—	—	—	†	—	—	—
Leoni	646	631	21	12	571	285	14	30
Martyrs	449	309	—	522	520	547	—	—
Mit Freuden Zart	604	423	415	—	—	522	20	4
Nicaea	162	160	36	223	1	266	251	26

[1] *English Hymnal* (1933).
[2] *Hymns Ancient and Modern* (1950).
[3] *Methodist Hymn Book* (1933).
[4] *Congregational Praise* (1951).
[5] *Church Hymnary* (1927).
[6] *The Hymnal* (1940) (U.S.A.).
[7] *The Pilgrim Hymnal* (1958) (U.S.A.).
[8] *The Methodist Hymnal* (1966) (U.S.A.).

† 77 in the *Scottish Psalter* (1929).
§ 146 in the *Scottish Psalter* (1929).
A—Appendix of tunes.

Appendices

	EH[1]	A&M[2]	M[3]	CP[4]	CH[5]	H[6]	P[7]	M[8]
Passion Chorale ..	102	111	202	127	107	75	170	418
Psalm 138	—	—	—	430	—	—	—	—
Rievaulx	—	164	38	192	5	—	—	—
St. Agnes	55A	515	289	—	422	24	240	516
St. Drostane	—	99	192	—	—	64	175	—
Surrey (Carey's) ..	491	179	349	67	172	306	—	—
There were Ninety and Nine	584	—	334	—	685	—	—	—
Uffingham	434	274	570	23	24	—	89	—
University	93	178	49	180	498	—	—	—
Vom Himmel Hoch (Erfurt)	17	151	126	78	156	22	121	281
York	472	301	347	156	§	312	95	—

BIBLIOGRAPHICAL NOTE

A list of all the works in which the reader might find part of
the data for this study would inevitably include all available works on Church History and on the History of Music.
Since bibliographies of Church History and of Musical History
will be found in the textbooks on those subjects it is not
necessary to repeat them here. The reader will be best
served by this brief bibliographical note, and by footnote-
references which we have given in the text.

For the pre-Christian period of ·musical speculation and
experience the reader is referred to the texts of Plato's
Republic and *Laws* and of Aristotle's *Politics* at the points
named in the footnotes to Chapter I.

For the Patristic period, the source is Migne's *Patrologia
Graeca* and *Patrologia Latina*, in the comprehensive Index
to which will be found numerous references under *Musica*.

For a general history of music related to social history, see
Paul Henry Láng, *Music in Western Civilisation*, first
published in America and available in England through
J. M. Dent & Sons (1942). For medieval music, see Gustav
Reese, *Music in the Middle Ages* also first published in
America and available here through Dent (1941). The
nineteenth century is excellently illuminated in Percy
Scholes, *The Mirror of Music*, 1844–1944 (Oxford University
Press and Novello, 1948).

The relations between music and Christian practice are dealt
with, in respect of their own periods, by Egon Wellesz,
A History of Byzantine Music and Hymnography (O.U.P.,
1949) and by Percy Scholes, *The Puritans and Music*
(O.U.P., 1936).

The general history of music may be read summarily but
accurately in Stanford and Forsyth, *A History of Music*
(O.U.P., ˋ1916) or in Alfred Einstein, *History of Music*
(Cassell, 1948).

Appendices

Church History is related to social civilisation most compre-prehensively in K. S. Latourette's monumental work *A History of the Expansion of Christianity*, first published in America and available here through Eyre and Spottis-woode (1939 *et sqq.*).

Beyond this it is only necessary to say that progressive research into the relations between music and Christian thought may be conducted by reading " between the lines " in the current periodicals of religious music societies.

Readers of my last chapter may care to be referred to other books in which I have pursued some of these themes further: *Twentieth Century Church Music* (Herbert Jenkins, 1964) goes into details about contemporary developments; *Words, Music and the Church* (Abingdon Press, to be published in 1968) examines the possibilities of further conversation between artists and the church especially in the field of drama; *Church Music and Theology* (S.C.M. Press, 1959) takes the question of practical theological judgment a little further. The matter of theology as an art is dealt with in *Into a Far Country* (Independent Press, 1962) and the history of hymns in *The Music of Christian Hymnology* (Independent Press, 1957).

INDEX

257

Index

Index

Index

Lully, J-B., 150
Luther, M., 113 f., 118, 154, 161

Machaut, G. de, 103, 117
Mackintosh, H. R., 202 n.
Macleod, Dr. G. F., 203
Maitland, J. A. Fuller, 203 n.
Mann, Michael, 252
Marcello, B., 156
Maritain, J., 203, 222 n.
Martial (Latin poet), 37
Martial (Musical school of), 97
Martin, F., 219
Mass in B minor (Bach), 156 f.,
    197
Mass in D (Beethoven), 104 n.,
    157, 197
Maunder, J. H., 181
Maurice, F. D., 170
Maxwell, W. D., 122
Melanchthon, P., 114, 121 f.
Methodism, Early, 158 ff.
Michelangelo, 110
Micklem, Dr. N., 5, 14 n.
Milan, Edict of, 42
Milton, J., 149
Modes, musical, in Plato, 22
Monody, 146 f.
Montanism, 71
Moody, D. L., 187, 204
Moravians, 155
Morley, T., 145
Morris, R. O., 179 n.
Muris, J. de, 105
Musica Encheiriadis, 99

Neale, J. M., 80 n.
Negro Spirituals, 188
Nero, 42
Nicene Creed, 217 n.
Nicholas I, Pope, 89
Notker Labeo, 83
Numeri (in Augustine), 52 ff.

Obrecht, J., 117
Ockham, William of, 111
Ockeghen, J. de, 117
Odington, W., 103 ff.
Odo of Cluny, 83

Old Testament, Music in, 15
Olivet to Calvary (Maunder), 181
Organum, 85 ff., 96 f., 99, 102,
    105 f., 211
Origen, 47, 51, 232
Orpheus, 17
Orr, E., 166 n.
"*Orthodoxy, European*," 146, 173 f.,
    205 f.
Ouseley, F. A. G., 180

Palestrina, G. P. da, 96, 116 f.,
    131 f., 145, 179, 192, 195
Palotta, M., 156
Parry, C. H. H., 208
Pastoral Symphony (Beethoven),
    252
Patrick, Millar, 55 n., 143 n.
Patrick, St., 71
Paul, St., 16
Paulus, L. Aemilius, 35
Pergolesi, G. B., 156
Peri, J., 116, 146 f.
Petrarch, 110
Philo, 46
Pietism, 154
Pisari, P., 156
Pius X, Pope, *Motu Proprio* of,
    1903, 194 ff., 213
Plato, 10, 18, 20 ff., 37, 55 f., 74,
    81, 100 f., 216, 220, 221
—*Laches*, 20 f.
—*Laws*, 23 ff.
—*Republic*, 21 ff., 29, 33
Plautus, 37
Pliny II, 46
Poole, R. Lane, 69 n.
Positivism, Logical, 205
Poulenc, F., 206
Prynne, W., 50
Psalm 1 (*Genevan*), 127
Psalm 138 (*Genevan*), 86
Psalmody-classes, 184
Psalters, English and Scottish, 143
Ptolemy, 81
Punic Wars, 36
Purcell, H., 149 f., 160, 209
Puritanism, 141 ff., 152 ff.
Pydna, Battle of, 35

260

Index

261

Index